The Original
Muffler Man

The Original Muffler Man

The Incredible story of
KASTURI LAL JAIN

SHUBHRA KRISHAN

HarperCollins *Publishers* India

First published in India by HarperCollins *Publishers* 2022
4th Floor, Tower A, Building No. 10, Phase II, DLF Cyber City,
Gurugram, Haryana – 122002
www.harpercollins.co.in

2 4 6 8 10 9 7 5 3 1

P-ISBN: 978-93-5489-225-7
E-ISBN: 978-93-5489-229-5

The views and opinions expressed in this book are the author's
own and the facts are as reported by her, and the publishers are not
in any way liable for the same.

Shubhra Krishan asserts the moral right
to be identified as the author of this work.

Cover design: Meena Rajasekaran
Front cover photo/Back cover photo: SP Vinod
Author photo: Nitin Gopal Srivastava

Typeset in 11.5/15.7 Adobe Jenson Pro (OTF) at
Manipal Technologies Limited, Manipal

Printed and bound at
Thomson Press (India) Ltd

❶ⓜ☺◗HarperCollinsIn

This book is produced from independently certified FSC® paper
to ensure responsible forest management.

Contents

Preface

———

*T*HE *Original Muffler Man* traces the inspirational journey of an individual from the remote town of Kasur (now in the Punjab region of Pakistan) to building an institution of global synergy. This is not a primer on how to build wealth, but an uplifting example of how to survive and thrive for almost a century while keeping ethics intact. We hope this book will act as a roadmap for entrepreneurs to pace their own professional journeys.

The story weaves its way around the hardships an individual goes through, and how the tough times inspire him to aspire even higher. Life is like a series of crests and troughs in the ocean. The challenge is to ride them out, reach the beautiful shore and build a ship so strong that our future generations can sail through with ease.

A special feature on Jainism in the book also explains how deep faith enables one to counter all challenges with maturity and perseverance.

A special thanks to Sandeep Kankariya, who has been instrumental in shaping the presentation of the book. My gratitude to Sathya Saran and Shubhra Krishan, who dived deep into the history of the Jain family and chronicled its fascinating journey.

This masterpiece is dedicated to all the present and future generations of entrepreneurs and managers, in the hope that they will find among its pages ideas, insights and inspiration to guide them, both in terms of conducting the self and business.

The company, Jain Amar, today is a testimony to the foundations laid down by the visionary, Sh Kasturi Lal Ji. The generations coming forward must strive to ensure that our hard-earned reputation for ethics and quality is maintained with each passing decade.

Akhil Jain

Introduction

— —

JAIN Amar is a family-owned clothing and accessories company. Founded in 1939 by Shri Chunni Lal Jain, they initially made simple men's accessories, such as woollen scarves and caps. Fast forward to the 21st century, and the company's complexion and scale have changed beyond belief! From the day they decided to diversify in the 1980s, their graph began to rise.

Today, Jain Amar provides affordable fast fashion to women, men, teenagers and children. Presented through three labels and counting, their products are sold in over 1,000 stores across three continents. From forecasting fashion trends to delivering cutting-edge styles, from retaining existing customers to acquiring new ones, this is one success story that deserves to be traced back to its modest roots.

The story you are about to read has been put together using quotes from Kasturi Lal Jain, his family members, friends and staff. The interviews with them were conducted in October 2020 at the Jain family home, their factory in Ludhiana and their office in Gurugram.

SECTION ONE

THE JOURNEY

1

How It All Began

_____

GREAT things, they say, have humble beginnings.

The remarkable story of Kasturi Lal Duggar Jain began more than 90 years ago in the small, sleepy town of Kasur in present-day Pakistan.

The second-youngest son of Chunni Lal Jain and Draupadi Devi, Kasturi Lal Duggar Jain arrived into the world in 1930. Theirs was, as was the norm back in those days, a fairly large family composed of six boys and two girls. Kasturi Lal's siblings were Amarnath, Prakash Chand, Rikhab Das, Gyan Chand, Jagdish, Shanti and Sheela.

Before we set foot into the man's journey, let us get to know the place where he lived, the life that he was born into and the simple events that set him on course.

Kasur is located some 32 kilometres from Lahore and about 137 kilometres from Ludhiana. The word "Kasur" means "palace" in Arabic. Interestingly, some historians say the name stems from Kush, the son of Lord Rama, who founded it. Be that as it may, Kasur lies to the south of Lahore, in the Pakistani province of Punjab. The city serves as the headquarters of Kasur district and is the 24th largest city in Pakistan by population. It is also known for being the burial place of the 17th-century Sufi poet Bulleh Shah.

But we are talking about the 1930s, when nothing much ever happened in Kasur. Of course, the rest of India was in the throes of turmoil. Led by Mahatma Gandhi, the struggle for Independence was steadily approaching its peak. Passive resistance was the form of protest chosen by the freedom fighters. They would often sit silently outside city halls, letting the brute forces of the British rain cane lashes on them until they fell unconscious.

Kasur, meanwhile, remained just that—a town called Kasur where daily life was as basic as could be. Those times were unimaginable in their modesty for the present generation. Good and safe roads were scarce in colonial India. Bullock carts were the favoured mode of transport.

Clothing was simple—dhoti-kurta and turban for the men and cotton saris for the women. Men pursued a small bunch of trades: you had blacksmiths, grocers, vegetable vendors, carpenters and such.

The place was dominated by the Khwajas, a well-polished Muslim community. A small cluster of Jains lived together in a separate area, but things were cordial between them and the Muslims. From time to time, they would exchange sweets on occasions such as weddings in the family.

Kasturi Lal's parents, both unschooled, ran a small grocery shop in Kasur. It fetched them a small amount, just enough to keep body and soul together. With each passing year, it became tougher and tougher to run a family of ten on their small earnings. Getting their children a good education was a wish, but all they could manage was to amass for them some knowledge of Hindi and Urdu.

The Great Depression that started in the US and caused a global economic slowdown had left a legacy of hunger and misery, making things even tougher. But we all know that storms leave sunshine in their wake, and often blessings come disguised as catastrophe.

Already, things had begun to look up—India was steadily building a strong railway network, and this single infrastructural element would have a far-reaching impact on the life of the country and its people.

One fine day, someone from Kasur—we don't know who—decided to fight the indigence. He boarded a train from Kasur and arrived in Ludhiana. In all probability, this was a person from a humble family engaged in a basic profession, much like

Chunni Lal Jain. Word must have travelled that the faraway pastures of the budding town were a brighter shade of green.

Ludhiana, located in the heart of modern-day Punjab, was a deep food bowl, filled to the brim with power-packed wheat. Its solid agrarian economy not only fed its own people but also became a key resource for battle-weary troops. Remember, World War II was already at our doorstep, and the kind of churning that must have been happening during those years can only be imagined.

Stepping into this atmosphere charged with both promise and dejection must have been exciting and intimidating in equal parts. Let's take a moment to visualise this unknown person's eyes widening as he stepped onto the platform at Ludhiana railway station, boggled at the sight of so many human beings at once.

But of course, the same determination that had propelled him to a new land also fuelled his journey onward. We shall never know of his trials and tribulations, but one thing is for sure: this person did find the town's pastures to be greener than those he had left behind.

Perhaps a bright and helpful kinsman or a new friend suggested selling woollens; winter in those days and in those parts used to be bone-chilling. Enterprising as he was, this person no doubt took the cue. Soon, he had crafted for himself a new life, and it was only a matter of time before he asked his family back home to board the train and join him in Ludhiana.

Word of this man's success reached all of Kasur and filtered into Kasturi Lal's home as well. We shall never know what month of the year or day of the month it was when the news reached their ears. Was the family sitting beside a crackling fire, warming themselves on a cold winter evening? Were they gathered around their small veranda, relying on cool breeze from the *neem* tree to beat the brutal heat? How well or little had they eaten that entire day?

No matter how simply or dramatically it was relayed, the message must have sounded like music to their penury-weary ears. Here it was at last, the prospect of changing life from bleak to bright!

By the time 1940 rolled in, Chunni Lal Jain had made up his mind. He sent two of his sons—Prakash Chand and Rikhab Das—to Ludhiana, hoping they would soon send good news.

Indeed, they did. And thereby begins a heart-warming tale.

2

Warming Up to Ludhiana

— —

BELIEVE it or not, Punjab began to see the beginnings of industrialisation more than 150 years ago. It started quietly, of course, after the famine of 1833 forced artisans from Kashmir to descend from the valley and settle in the plains of Punjab. Amritsar and Ludhiana, in particular, saw large numbers of these artisans.

The knitwear industry began to come into its own in the year 1902, when the first hand-woven knits unit was set up in the city. The very next year, most manufacturers switched to imported hand-operated machinery.

India was still under the British rule, so woollen products from Kashmir became *cashmere*, and most of the high-quality stuff was exported to Europe. Premium Pashmina shawls were a hot favourite and remain so to this day.

During the early part of the 20th century, industrialisation picked up pace, and new hosiery machines were installed. Probably the first knitted product to be made with the machines was socks, followed by woollen scarves that came to be known as mufflers.

There were no elaborate business plans made, nor too many calculations done. All that the Jain family needed was to find a spot where they could set up shop, and they did. It was a small, boxy little structure, nearly concealed by a huge pipal tree. It stands there to this day, a touching testament to the diligence of a man who believed in the power of hard work.

Kasturi Lal Jain puts it simply: "Someone suggested mufflers would be a good business to start, because they were useful in keeping people warm in the chilly winters of Punjab. Thick cotton was cheap and available in plenty in those times. Hand-operated muffler-knitting machines were inexpensive too. So we bought one machine and started making mufflers."

The family moved to Ludhiana in stages—first Prakash Chand and Rikhab Das, then two more brothers, then the parents, and finally the remaining siblings. They lived together, right where the shop was. Their extended family in Kasur slowly moved to Faridkot and settled there.

"In those times, you could buy a good-quality muffler for just three rupees," shares Jain. Their mufflers, made by hand with utmost attention to detail, began to sell well. During World War II, the knitwear industry got a boost due to the increasing requirements of hosiery items by the defence forces.

Kasturi Lal was still a child of 10 when the family business started. He had just completed his 4th grade in Kasur, and his father was keen to educate him well. So, he was enrolled in the SAN Jain School on Daresi Road in Ludhiana, where he studied until the 8th grade, and then shifted to SDP School in the 9th grade.

Stray memories of his school days fill his eyes as he travels back in time. SAN Jain School was strict on discipline. One of his teachers there would always keep sharing nuggets of advice that stayed with him throughout his life: keep your nails short, never trim your nose hair, always change your clothes after going back home from school.

At SDP School, his headmaster's name was Mr. Baljeet Singh Khosla. In the 10th grade, one of his friends was Sat Pal Singh Mittal, a good boy who was weak in studies. The master would make him stand on the bench as soon as he arrived. "But I will always remember him as a good soul. He was a brilliant orator and always ready to help the community. Sadly, he died young," says Kasturi Lal, his eyes misting over.

The year 1946 dawned, and it was time for Kasturi Lal to enter college. "In those days, we had no clue where to study or what subject to take," he recalls. "We had heard of Arya College, which was pretty famous, but its reputation was that only the non-serious crowd took admission there. So, I enrolled in the government college. The procedure was fairly simple. You just went to the window, submitted a form and got admission. I opted to study Economics, Politics, Urdu, Mathematics, Hindi and English."

Slowly, he made new friends. Most of them would walk back home from college. It took a few months for him to settle into college, mostly because the new sense of freedom was both exciting and a bit disconcerting. Gone were the days of being constantly monitored. In college, the professors were not really bothered about students and their shenanigans. Students were left to study by themselves, and there were quite a few free periods. Since they were free to do as they pleased, Kasturi Lal and his friends would often walk down to a friend's home and munch on fresh carrots and radishes. And if they were in the mood for a special treat, there was always the famous dahi samosa from Khushi Ram Mithai Shop.

Among Kasturi Lal's close friends was a boy called Baldev Kapoor. They would often walk down to Jagraon Bridge, buying sugarcane on the way. They always made sure to take turns to pay for the little treat. For hours, the two youngsters would sit and chat, munching on the juicy sugarcane and talking about life.

The chief administrator of the college, Mr. I.M. Verma, was a good man with a laid-back attitude to life. "He seemed to live in his own world, to the extent that he often came to class with his shirt buttons done all wrong! Later, we got to know that he was crazy about a girl…"

Speaking of girls, it was not common for boys and girls to study together. There was a time when one girl started coming to their college to attend economics lectures. And because of her, all the boys were suddenly at their best behaviour!

Of course, all of college life was not fun and freedom. The nation was inching closer and closer to Independence, and Ludhiana was not Kasur—the impact of it all was being felt hugely in the city. Kasturi Lal remembers 1947 as a year of terrifying turmoil, peppered with riots among Hindus and Muslims. Thankfully, the Deputy Commissioner of Ludhiana was a very capable man, one who managed to keep tempers down on both sides.

But it wasn't easy at all. "I remember Hindus standing on one side of Chowra Bazaar, watching the Muslims leave en masse…" Camps were set up for people coming in from Pakistan, and students were asked to volunteer. Kasturi Lal and his friends put their heart and soul into assisting the new immigrants during this tough period.

In 1950, he graduated from college in the first division. "I was over the moon," says Kasturi Lal, beaming. "Three or four of us rushed to Khushi Ram's shop and tucked into lots of mithai. I still remember my friend Vishwamitra, who was quite a smart cookie. Each time the bill came, he would excuse himself to go to the loo!"

These random memories come to Kasturi Lal in charming bits and pieces. It is endearing that he remembers these bitter-sweet episodes, sometimes with surprising clarity.

He remembers how Hindus and Muslims lived in separate parts of Ludhiana back then. "Hindus to the left, and Muslims to the right, so to say." There was a small community of Jains, among whom the Aggrawal Jains were quite prosperous. It was a time of brotherhood and bonhomie, with people stepping up without hesitation to help each other in times of difficulty.

"But help was never given as charity or donation," he points out. "It was done in the gentlest manner, in the guise of a gift for the family. Today, the world is a changed place. Even blood brothers refuse to help each other in times of need," he observes with a sigh.

In his own family, the spirit of sibling love was strong. They worked together as a unit, with money being shared by everyone. Their father, Chunni Lal Jain, was the glue that held them all together. The women of the family not only ran house smoothly but also contributed to the growing business by knitting tassels on the mufflers.

The exemplary practice they followed was to pay the ladies of the house for the work they did. With the money they earned, these wise women bought jewellery for their children's future weddings.

Then, Kasturi Lal's graduation was complete. He was now a strapping young man, qualified and ready to take on the world. But first, his personal life was on the brink of a major event—marriage.

3

A Partnership for Life

— —

No matter how far apart two people are from each other, destiny has a way of bringing their lives together. In those days, a 300-kilometre distance was not an easy five-hour drive in the comfort of a luxury car on a four-lane highway. But fate seamlessly introduced Kasturi Lal to the woman who was to be united in holy matrimony with him.

He still remembers how the match was made. "I did have a slight defect in my foot. But the highly revered Jain saints Maharaj Shri Phool Chand Ji, Shri Shanti Swarup Ji, Shri Sumati Prakash Ji, who were present at Jain Nagar in Meerut, encouraged the girl's family to accept me as their son-in-law."

Sitting in her Ludhiana mansion today, Kamla Jain radiates grace. She has the countenance of a woman who has led a fulfilled life. She was born in 1933, and her journey with Kasturi Lal Jain began in 1952. In the nearly seven decades since then, she has been his constant companion in all of life's ups and downs, highs and lows.

While her own recollections of childhood are hazy, she has clear memories of their time in Sialkot, Pakistan, where they lived until six months before the Partition. The family had their own rubber factory and a comfortable home in Sialkot, but, like thousands of others, they crossed over to the Indian side in search of a safe new abode. Kamla was just 14 years old then.

It wasn't an easy move and had to be done in careful instalments. It was decided that Kamla's father and her elder brother and his wife would stay back in Pakistan while the rest of the family set out and arrived in Jammu. From there they headed to Amritsar, and onward to Alwar, where her maternal uncle's in-laws lived. "They were very wealthy, but more than that, they had a richness of heart that is not easy to find," Kamla recalls. "They threw open the doors of their *dharamshalas* and residences for us, without charging us a single penny of rent. Not only that, they provided each family with six months' worth of ration—how can I ever forget their generosity!"

While they made Alwar their temporary home for two years, the patriarch of the family moved his operations from Sialkot to Katni in Madhya Pradesh. The rubber-making machines were moved all the way, and operations restarted with full gusto. The rubber factory is functional to this day.

This may sound simple when written down in a paragraph. But imagine a large joint family, plucked from its birthplace and compelled to leave its roots and legacy behind. Add to this the lack of strong infrastructure, and the sheer enormity of a distant move into a place they could not call their own, and the picture at once grows grim. But then the people of that generation rode over the crests and troughs of life with practised ease. They lived on the assumption that hard work was a way of life; nothing was too much trouble in their book.

By 1952, however, Kamla Jain's family was well settled in Meerut, thanks to their Guruji. He identified and guided them to purchase a huge stretch of land, realising it would be an ideal settlement for the 400-odd immigrant Jain families. Of these a majority were from Rawalpindi, and a small number from Sialkot and Kasur. Anyhow, they were all rehabilitated as one community, which was christened Jain Nagar, and life began afresh.

Business was growing, and Kamla was studying in college. She had done her high school in Sialkot. There were no board exams then, and the 10th grade degree was called *Ratan* and high school level degree was called *Bhushan*. She had got her books along from Pakistan and continued her education, mostly in Hindi, with a bit of Urdu and very little English— just enough for her to sign her name. While she pursued a *Prabhakar* degree, equivalent to today's graduation, marriage prospects for her began coming in. Because the Jain community had networks throughout the country, word about the Meerut Jains' family reached the Ludhiana Jains.

Kasturi Lal Jain's sister, Sheela, travelled to Meerut to see the girl under some pretext. She liked her and gave the green signal. That was enough for the family to give its approval—after all, Sheela was a beloved sister to six brothers, and the apple of everyone's eye.

Chunni Lal Jain took a *baarat* of 50 relatives and friends from Ludhiana to Meerut. Kamla's father, who had by now built a great reputation in the Jain community, was a member of some exclusive clubs. Other members of the clubs stepped forward to welcome the groom's side, and a fleet of cars was sent to the railway station to pick them up and bring them to their accommodation.

On the day of the wedding, some of Kamla's friends took a sneak peek at Kasturi and came running to her. "The boy is very good looking," they said. The young bride blushed delightedly. The wedding was conducted according to traditional Jain rituals and, by the end of the evening, they were bonded forever as man and wife.

Kasturi Lal remembers that the muffler business was in the ascendant when he got married. "In fact, it was so hectic that we had more orders than we could handle. So, the very day we returned to Ludhiana, I headed straight for the shop. Those days, working late nights was the norm for me, and my wife was fully supportive of my efforts."

One memory from her early days of marriage comes back to Kamla often. "We had a family Pandit*ji* who lived in Delhi.

He had predicted a beautiful life for me. So, when he came visiting, I jokingly asked him what happened to his prediction that I would have a bungalow and cars and wealth. He put mine and my husband's hands on his knee and said solemnly, "You will have them all. I promise you."

Panditji passed away just 15 days after Kamla's marriage. But every one of his words came true.

4

Knitting a Future Together

— —

WHEN Kamla arrived in Ludhiana, Kasturi Lal's family owned a small shop and lived in a rented home. She was welcomed warmly into her new household and came to admire the diligent spirit of her young husband, then only about 21 years old.

Knit by knit, the muffler business grew. The high quality of the products made them easy to sell, even across long distances. It was no cakewalk, of course. Most days, Kasturi Lal left home by 8 a.m. and returned from the shop only at 4 in the morning. His father would wait outside the house in the veranda for his son, and only when he returned would they both go inside. But eating their meals at home was important to them, and Kasturi Lal would almost always come home for lunch, if not also for dinner. Food was never served cold. If three family members came home at three different times, each one was given fresh, hot food.

Soon, Kamla realised that generosity was a way of life for her in-laws. Every day, her father-in-law would get one kilo of *atta* kneaded to make *rotis* for feeding beggars and stray dogs. He would get his daughter to stitch undergarments to donate to the poor. "It was so wonderful that he cared in these small, simple ways," says Kamla.

Combined with this largeness of heart, the family's diligence and persistence paid off. Slowly, they were able to earn enough to purchase their own house. "The milk of four buffaloes would come into our house. We never had to buy milk, yoghurt, butter or ghee from outside, ever."

Kamla took some time adjusting to life in Ludhiana. She missed Meerut and reported to her family and friends that her new city was not as clean and beautiful. But it was all compensated for by the affectionate atmosphere at home.

Looking back, she remembers her father- and mother-in-law as gentle, open-minded people who came from a very traditional background but never tried to suppress or dominate her. One small gesture that touched her was that her father-in-law allowed her to wear the winter coat she had got from her father as a gift at the time of her wedding. In Punjab those days, women didn't wear coats—only shawls. But though her father-in-law never allowed anyone else in the family to wear coats, he told his son, "My *bahu's* father has gifted her a coat. Tell her to wear it if she wants." She never forgot that kindness and recalls it as one of the key things that showed how open-hearted he was.

In other matters, too, there were very few restrictions on her and the other women in the family. "I would visit my *maika* two to three times a year. The Frontier Mail ran in the evenings, directly from Ludhiana to Meerut, so it was quite convenient, too."

Back home in Meerut, women never kept the *ghooghat* in front of men. But here, Kamla had to drape her *sari pallu* over her face as a sort of *purdah* from the older men in the family. In fact, before her marriage, she had always worn *salwar-kameez*. But this was Ludhiana, and saris were worn quite regularly. Initially, the young woman found it difficult to drape the garment correctly, but she soon not only grew accustomed to it but started liking the grace and beauty of the sari.

With increasing prosperity, the daughters-in-law of the house began getting jewellery made. Once, her father-in-law remarked that it might be a better idea to save cash, but she politely told him that gold was essential. After all, they had three children who would need to be married off.

In those days, people began their day by going to the Jain Sthanak, where monks would deliver their daily discourse. "It was unthinkable for a trader to open his shop without the *darshan* of his Guruji," she recalls.

Her in-laws were as respectful of religion as her family had been back home, which helped Kamla adjust easily. When her own sons got married, she never had to tell her daughters-in-law to practise their daily rituals. Each new bride observed and learned without much effort.

Speaking of rituals, the Shwetamabar Jains spend 48 minutes—ideally in the morning—doing Samayik, which is a period devoted to spiritual thinking. During this time, they cover their faces with masks, just like their Gurus, and do the rosary while chanting the *Namokar Mantra*. Today, having fulfilled all her household duties, Kamla practises Samayik several times a day. You can read more about the daily practice of Samayik in the special section on Jainism in this book.

As a new bride, Kamla found her husband to be a man of few words. She, on the other hand, was a chirpy, jovial person, and got along well with her in-laws. It was a full house, with not only her father- and mother-in-law but also their sons and daughters-in-law. She does not remember a single conflict in the family; they lived in peace and harmony.

We tend to assume that family life in those days was rather difficult for a woman. Perhaps conditioned by what we see in old Hindi movies, we imagine new brides sweating it out in the kitchens, controlled by fierce mothers-in-law. But prepare to be pleasantly surprised! For one full year, Kamla was not even allowed to go into the kitchen. This was a simple but beautiful tradition in the Jain household—one that even some "modern" families could draw inspiration from.

After three years of marriage, Kasturi Lal and Kamla became parents to Sunil, followed by Bipan after five years and a daughter after seven years. Kasturi Lal was keen for his children to study in convent schools. While the eldest son did his schooling in Ludhiana, the plan was to send Bipan to a boarding school in Dehradun. Soon, however, a convent school opened in Ludhiana itself, and he was called back and enrolled in it.

Kamla addresses Kasturi Lal as Daddy*ji*, just like everyone else in the family.

With time, Kasturi Lal Jain has eased himself out of the day-to-day running of the business. His sons Bipan and Sunil Jain leave home early in the morning and return only in the evening. It continues to be a busy life, just as Kamla has always known it.

5

The Years of Growth

— —

THE '50s and '60s saw a steady rise in the family business. The year 1955, in particular, proved to be a good one.

While any business grows directly in proportion to the hard work and sincerity put in by the entrepreneurs, devotion to dharma and a strong spirit of giving back to society generates good karma. This has always been the guiding principle in Kasturi Lal Jain's family.

Sometime in the 1950s, Sadhvi Shri Lajjawati Ji Maharaj and Shri Abhay Kumari Ji Maharaj were at the Ludhiana Jain Sthanak. Kasturi Lal and Kamla visited them often for *darshan*. One lady, who was a community worker in the same campus, had some savings with her. On Maharaj ji's instruction, she handed over a sum of Rs 10,000 to Kasturi Lal, to be kept aside. Kasturi Lal felt a bit tense that a monthly interest of Rs 100 would now begin.

Miraculously, the sum became highly instrumental in the growth of the business. Eleven months later, the saints called Kasturi Lal. They asked him to bring the money back and give it to the lady the following day.

Kasturi Lal's principles did not allow him to accept favours from anyone for too long. He had already carried the amount in his pocket when visiting the Sthanak. He immediately returned the sum without hesitation. His attitude and honest intentions further impressed everyone. The Maharaj happily gave her sermon and recited an auspicious mantra called the *mangal path* to them.

The biggest markets for Kasturi Lal Jain's mufflers were Delhi, Uttar Pradesh and, most importantly, Bihar. Interestingly, the demand for the woollen scarf was huge in Bihar because it was customary to gift mufflers and umbrellas at weddings.

In proportion to the increasing manufacturing, the work hours grew too. Kasturi Lal and his brothers would leave home early in the morning and work at the factory until about 10 p.m. After that, they would return to the shop and carefully sort the orders they had received, bundling each one into small packets. The next morning, the cycle would begin all over again.

There were both pros and cons of expanding the trade. For big orders, it became necessary to assess the reliability of the customer, and also to travel far. The smaller orders brought in less money but could be handled locally. With each transaction and each interaction, the brothers gained a little more experience and insights into human nature.

In those days, mufflers were made from spun cotton, on simple machines. Slowly, raw material began to be imported. The Oswal family, a known name in the hosiery business, were the first to import. This benefited the entire community.

With growth come changes, and the Jain family was no different. There came a point when they decided it was time to segregate their shop and their home, which had so far run jointly. So, the small shop was shifted to Dal Bazaar. Throughout the day, customers would walk in and out of the shop. Those were the heydays of Jain Amar, full of activity and very rewarding financially as well as mentally.

Since their home was still located close to the shop, Jain Amar's customers would be served tea and snacks from home. In those days of social-media-free living, interpersonal relations were real and beautiful. Some people grew closer to them with time. One such customer was the family of Shri Hukum Chand Jain, who belonged to Nepal. They were often invited home and served a hearty meal of *paranthas* and *lassi*. Looking after one's guests was considered not only one's duty but a privilege.

Long after the customers had left, the family would stay up and pack all the goods, sometimes working late past midnight. Even the ladies of the house worked 20 hours a day, looking after both the home and the business. The mufflers were mostly spun at home only. This was a common practice in most of the shops and households in Ludhiana.

Slowly, it was time to change the house too. Mandibagh Khazanchi seemed to be a good location, and they shifted there. Now, with things moving along at a smooth pace, they were able to afford a few buffaloes. Every day, Kasturi Lal Jain's father would come home at 11 a.m. from the shop to feed the cattle. They hired a servant, too. The entire discipline and routine of the house was in their father's charge.

Kasturi Lal's mother liked to cook every meal with her own hands. She would make such beautifully puffed and delicate *phulkas* that visiting sadhus and sadhvis liked to accept them from her hands. A few extra *rotis* were always cooked for the stray dogs of the neighbourhood.

In 1960, the family moved to yet another house, this time in Wait Gunj. The streak of good luck continued. In fact, one of those years in the 1960s was particularly cold. The sun did not make an appearance for two weeks. People shivered in the brutal cold and the demand for woollen products jumped multiple-fold. Mufflers, caps, gloves—sellers began making them at breakneck pace, even using leftover material to quickly stitch them up. Those were profitable times for the Jain family.

"From the beginning, our focus was always on the customers," says Kasturi Lal. "Even their slightest complaint was attended to immediately. This established a relationship of trust with our buyers, and went a long way in consolidating our reputation."

6

Changing Relationships

— —

People think money will bring happiness, but the truth is that money can also complicate relationships. While the Jain family's muffler business steadily picked up and the Kasur days of penury became a distant memory, the times ahead were set to grow turbulent.

Subtle hiccups in personal equations began to rear their head as the profits grew and families expanded. Year by year, the disquiet grew a little more, starting with slow rumbles of discontent. Rikhab Das was the first to suggest a parting of ways. Soon, the same murmurs began emerging from Prakash Chand. Outwardly, the bonhomie continued, but there descended an unmistakable shadow of restlessness in their hearts.

One of the brothers, Gyan Chand, was diagnosed with a hole in his heart. In those days, there was very little knowledge of and no cure for ailments of this kind. Even the diagnosis of his illness was made not by a doctor but by his school master. Gyan Chand was a good, honest soul and the family put him in charge of maintaining the shop accounts. He did so with utmost sincerity. Until about 1965, he discharged this responsibility, then his health deteriorated and he bid a quiet goodbye to the world.

The business was still in its infancy, and account-keeping was simple and straightforward. So, it did not take much for the brothers to settle the finances among themselves. But human nature being what it is, an unrelated observer began creating unnecessary tension by suggesting that they erect a straight wall to partition the shop itself.

"People will always poke their nose into things that don't concern them, but we as a Jain community and as a solid family never allowed their opinions to influence our decisions," Kasturi Lal asserts.

The parting of ways presented the issue of what to do with the shop that they had, but they had faith that things would turn out well. That was because the location of the shop had been recommended to them by a Jain saint of great repute.

And sure enough, the problems seemed to solve themselves. Kasturi Lal Jain remembers facing a big roadblock—his brother Prakash Chand wanted to keep the entire shop for himself. It was a very successful shop, but the time had come to divide it. According to the existing laws, the primary owner had the first right over the entire shop, and Prakash Chand was the primary owner. But that is when fate and the blessings of the saints intervened. On the day that one part of the family was to leave the shop and move away, there came a government ruling that cancelled the old law and allowed the shop to remain with Kasturi Lal's family.

At first, Kasturi Lal was very reluctant to take over the shop. It had been shut for quite some time, and there was a pipal tree on the premises. It was an old structure, with thick 28-inch walls. Chipping away at it, they managed to create more space in the shop. On the right side, a door was created, which led out to an open compound, filling the inside with natural light. But the structure of the shop was such that even after expansion, it fell short of even a decent seven-foot height. Kasturi Lal then asked a lawyer relative of his, Shri Tek Chand, to help restructure the shop, so that he could mediate things peacefully, avoiding any further conflict in the family.

The final touches to the reconstruction were given by a mason and a local painter. Pandit Kishan Lal was invited from Delhi to inaugurate the shop formally.

There was a well outside the shop, where people used to come and bathe. Some people in the *mohalla* objected that the bathers would be uncomfortable with the shop door opened, so that had to be closed.

The pipal tree continued to stand on the platform of the shop, of course. The locals worshipped it. The shop proved to be lucky for the family, and business grew manifold.

Looking back on that period, Kasturi Lal Jain is visibly accepting of the fact that change is a part of life, and, all said and done, theirs has been a fulfilling journey. The shop still stands in the heart of Ludhiana, and the address is still Pipal Building. Some things do remain unchanged, and thank God for that.

7

Bridging the Generation Gap

— —

Kasturi Lal Jain has built his enterprise literally by the labour of his hands. He has seen days of abject penury and optimum comfort. The difference between the two, he knows, is one and only one—money. It is your relationship with money that can mean the difference between failure and success, frustration and elation.

Of course, as is the case with most family-owned businesses, there comes a point when two schools of thought find themselves at odds with each other in the money-management department. The Jain family has seen its own share of those differences.

But there's a refreshing difference in their approach to this difference of opinion. Thanks to their solid bonding, deep understanding and firm religious beliefs, they are, to this day, able to communicate with each other without rancour, always keeping the larger picture in mind.

For example, the family's practice of sitting together every evening, discussing the day's events and updating each other on work done and plans made, allows them to talk threadbare about their ideas and viewpoints. The presence of Kasturi Lal Jain as their patriarch is immensely reassuring, since he symbolises experience and wisdom.

"We may not always agree, but we are able to see where each of us is coming from, and that I think is very healthy, because it allows us to address only specific issues rather than get into egoistic battles," shares his grandson Akhil Jain.

One area of disagreement, for example, is bank loans. Being a traditional businessman, Kasturi Lal Jain neither understands nor approves of the need to borrow from banks. In his time, a loan was taken on a personal basis, in good faith, and returning it was a commitment that no self-respecting person would default on.

"Today, banks charge you huge amounts of interest. I would never get into a borrowing cycle with them," he declares.

No matter what the disagreement, though, his sons and grandsons never fail to share everything with him. Even today, every new sample and design is first shown to him for his opinion and approval, even though he is essentially a traditional muffler expert.

It was Kasturi Lal's son Bipan Jain who chose the name "Madame" for their growing enterprise, when they began making fashion garments for women. Kasturi Lal approved of the brand name. "It is a French word for ladies; Madame with an 'e,'" he says, with unmistakable pride. "I liked it instantly."

There is another staunch pillar that keeps the family grounded and realistic. And that is their deliberate exposure to hardship. Never have they taken their success and its accompanying comforts for granted.

"When I came back from Delhi after a fantastic exposure to the real world in NIFT, I was sort of walking on air," recalls Akhil. "Studying in a glamorous, modern institute of such repute does that to you."

But his father brought him back to reality by handing him the keys to the Dal Bazaar shop, where his duty was to deal with customers day in and day out. Akhil would offer them water, take their orders and ensure that they were packaged properly, after which he would personally deliver the orders. It was all hands-on wholesale work, and every dealing was in cash. He did this for six months, after which his father told him he was ready to move to the factory and take on bigger responsibilities.

At the factory, Akhil's first task was to "tame the loose horses," as he puts it. "I guess anybody young and full of ideas would do the same—it is natural to find flaws in the old system and want to rectify them at a fast pace. I am sure my children would want to do the same," he says philosophically.

Bipan Jain, his uncle, held the prime position at the factory. Akhil reported to him. At some point, he wanted to prove himself capable of taking charge, but he knew it would take time. It did. Four years of rigorous work. And as soon as he sat on that chair, he realised what massive responsibility it meant—it was a hot seat, quite literally!

Not one to be daunted, Akhil busied himself trying to change the antiquated systems that existed. "Our transactions at that time were recorded in too basic a manner," he says. "I brought in ERP, a system that helps you to collect financial data from various departments to create reports and financial statements."

But it wasn't easy. His father, accustomed to his own ad hoc way of functioning, was initially against paying for the 15 or so licences that ERP required. According to him, the existing system was working just fine. Akhil understood his father's resistance and waited it out patiently. It took nearly two years for Sunil Jain to be finally convinced, but once the ERP was functional, its precision and convenience spoke for itself.

This is how, bit by slow bit, the older generation began to concede, realising that work was expanding and needed to be streamlined for faster results and more efficient flow.

"Moving forward, I have a definite plan for my life. I would like to retire from business at the age of 55 and dedicate myself to charity and social causes. But to be able to do that, there has to be enough to give away. This is what Jainism teaches us—earn and then give. All our Tirthankaras were *chakravarti* rajas who gave away their wealth and worldly belongings," says Akhil.

8

The Foundations of Faith

Today, Kasturi Lal Jain is a highly respected member of the Jain community. A testament to this is the fact that when the 12th President of India, Smt Pratibha Patil, conferred the title of *Raj Rishi* on Muni Sumti Prakashji, it was Kasturi Lal who received it on his behalf.

This immense dedication to faith took root when, at the tender age of two, Kasturi Lal Jain developed a problem in his foot.

In those days, most ailments were hard to diagnose and treat. And in any case, Kasur had almost non-existent medical facilities.

The child was in severe pain, so the parents took him to Lahore, covering a long distance in a bullock cart. However, the hospital in Lahore was crammed, and not much attention was given to non-Muslim patients.

Dejected, they rode back home. On the way, someone suggested they take a detour to visit a Jain saint who was known to have healing powers. Having nothing to lose, they agreed. The saint looked at the child's foot and recited a mantra. He did not even touch the foot.

A day or two later, the foot was healed. It was a miracle.

This incident remains firmly etched in Kasturi Lal's mind to this day. He points to his foot, remarking that it has always been his weak point, and that it is probably smaller than the other one.

But thanks to the healing he received from the saint, he was not only able to walk but also go for long runs. "I have always loved to exercise," he says. "And in my childhood, I would cross a huge nullah and run barefoot on wet grass for miles, along with my brothers."

After this episode, the family began to place its faith in Jain saints. The more they observed and followed, the more they believed.

And so it continues to this day.

Kasturi Lal can recall dozens of incidents and events that deepened his faith in the power of Jain wisdom. He recounts some of them:

"When I was in college, my *Mamaji* invited a saint. We were working in the factory then, so we offered to let him stay the night there. He readily agreed. During the course of the evening, he spoke to our workers and asked them if they were happy. Each one of them said they were satisfied with both the work and their employer. This brought a smile to his face.

"Later, before going to bed, the saint asked me to make a wish. My exams had just ended, and I said I would very much like to pass in the first division. He blessed me. The next day, my results came—and I had a first division.

"Another time, a Maharaj was staying with us and my father was expected back from the village. It was lunch time, and he said he would like to wait for my father to join us. But after about five to ten minutes, he suddenly said there was no point waiting, as my father would take time negotiating with the porters at the railway station. We were astonished when our father came back late and told us this was exactly what had held him up!"

The advice of Jain saints turned out to be extremely beneficial for the business as well. They seemed to have a divine instinct for recommending the right decisions at the right time. "For example, my father was worried that two of his sons had to be married off and gold prices were shooting through the roof. The Maharaj advised him to wait it out for just a while, and sure enough, the prices came down to normal. Similarly, he advised us to buy as much raw material for muffler-making as we could. As soon as we had bought it, the prices almost doubled overnight."

In the 1970s, a man from Siwan sent a court warrant to Kasturi Lal Jain, alleging that he was owed some money.

This was a complete hoax, prevalent in those times. "I was extremely perturbed and went to Meerut to meet Shanti Swarup Maharaj ji along with my wife Kamla. He reassured us saying that we had nothing to worry about. One day before our court appearance, we went to our accuser's place and had breakfast with him.

"And on the date of the case, I observed a strict fast. We appeared before the judge, who heard the arguments on both sides and dismissed the case. I was so relieved! We took the first bus—it was headed to Kathmandu. We stayed there one day and then left for home. On the sixth day, with the blessings of Maharaj Shri Ji, we reached safely. My wife Kamla, who had been fasting rigorously for the last seven days, greeted us with tears of joy."

Now, nearly 90 years since the foot healed, the Jain family still travels across the country to pay its respects to the saints. And while this may sound like a simple enough thing to do, the truth is, each trip involves a considerable amount of travel as well as physical discomfort.

Let us travel with them to the interiors of Jodhpur, Rajasthan.

The month is January, and the freezing breeze seems to stab you, like a thousand sharp needles. It is 2021, and the world is still in shock after the onslaught of the coronavirus.

Delhi airport is definitely not what it used to be; everywhere, there are masks, sanitisers and PPE kits. People stare at each other a bit warily, but flights must be taken and tasks must be accomplished. Everyone is doing the best they can.

On one such wintry morning, three members of the Jain family set out to meet their revered saints, who are currently in the vicinity of Jodhpur.

The flight leaves and arrives on time, but not a minute is spent in the big city. They leave by road, juddering through the cold desert landscape for two hours, then turn into a dusty road off the highway. Except for the odd herd of goats and motorbikes, the stretch is quite empty.

Google Maps directs them to a village, crammed with houses painted light blue and mauve. The streets here are narrow as windpipes. A bull stands outside a gate, receiving its daily feed from the owners. Soon, it will move away to another home, where the occupants will offer him another meal.

This is how Jain mendicants also receive their offerings. The practice is called *gochari*, which means gathering food in the manner that a cow does.

This evening, the saints have been welcomed into a home in the village of Patwa. Composed of various ages, they are travelling in a batch of seven. The accommodation for the night is as basic as can be, but then saints of the order allow themselves no attachment to material comforts.

The Jain family, on the other hand, is by now established in the fashion trade and lives a life of plenty and luxury in Ludhiana. Surely, the dust and general grime of this small village must be bothersome?

But no. With utmost ease and humility, they bow before the eldest of the saints, Muni Sumti Prakash Ji. They are overwhelmed with devotion and emotion at the very sight of him.

Settling down at the great man's feet, Akhil Jain and his mother Neelam Jain receive his blessings. The Muni inquires after the family's health and sends his good wishes to Akhil's ailing *dadi* over a video call. Akhil opens a large suitcase that he has carried all the way from Ludhiana. It is filled with clothing for the wandering saints—beautiful mufflers, shawls and *asanas* for them to meditate on.

The saint accepts the gifts with a smile.

Afterwards, the villagers serve them a rural meal, and it is enjoyed sitting on *daris* inside a structure that looks like an exposed brick hall with a corner that serves as its kitchen.

They spend some more time at the feet of their beloved saints and then head to a Jain *dharamshala* which is located some five hours away from Patwa, in a place called Nakoda. The Nakodaji Parasvanath Temple is an iconic *tirtha* for Jains.

The *dharamshala* provides a room lined with four beds. It is spotless and has a geyser, AC and western-style WC. But there are no amenities such as water, soap and towel. The blankets provided are rather thin for the weather.

But the family, having spent several nights in *dharamshalas*, has come prepared with everything they require. Not a murmur escapes them about the discomfort of travel or the compromises it requires. Faith is uppermost in their minds, and they cannot wait to rise early and visit the temple yet another time.

The beauty of the Jain family lifestyle is that their faith is not limited to visiting saints and temples.

In their daily life, they practise the essentials of Jain tenets, as have been advised for householders to follow. Among these are:

Samayik: Samayik is one of the most important ritual practices of Jainism, during which we try to come closer to our soul. During samayik, we sit down in one place, ideally for 48 minutes. For this time, we isolate ourselves from our daily household, social, business or school activities and read religious books, pray, worship, recite rosary or meditate.

Pratikraman: This is a daily evening ritual during which Jains do *prayaschit*, or ask forgiveness for their sins and hurtful actions committed knowingly or unknowingly during the day. This daily introspection is a wonderful way to self-assess and self-correct. It brings peace of mind and positivity, helping us to sleep with a clear conscience and a light heart.

Self-discipline: This is practised in the form of giving up one thing every day. It could be something as simple as cardamom. Resolving to go without one item daily helps us build willpower and practise moderation.

Fasting: Many members of Kasturi Lal Jain's family, including the teenagers, observe a partial or full fast at regular intervals. For years on end, until his health permitted, Kasturi Lal himself spent many days when he would eat just a handful of *chana* during the entire day. Tuesdays are salt-free days for Akhil Jain, who credits his grandmother for inspiring him to follow dietary discipline.

Kasturi Lal Jain recalls an amusing incident related to his practice of samayik. "Once, a gentleman came to meet me and was told I was busy doing samayik. He looked absolutely shocked. Later, I got to know that he had misunderstood 'samayik' as being 'smack'!"

9

Travel Tales

— —

Ask Kamla to pick one memorable phase from her married life and she says, without hesitation, that it was their travels together, which brought them closer and enriched their horizons. She is grateful to her husband for having taken her along across continents, showing her the glorious world in all its beauty.

The business of mufflers was a seasonal one, so for about six months, there would be no work. That period of leisure gave Kasturi Lal and Kamla the perfect opportunity to travel for a good two months, which both of them loved equally. Even today, Kamla's face lights up at the memory of those trips.

Their first flight abroad was to Singapore, where they were to meet one of her brother's friends. At the airport, they realised no one had come to pick them up. A bit disappointed, they somehow found their way to their host's place.

Very soon, it was clear to them that the hosts were not too pleased to have them over. "The lady of the house served us tea and snacks, then disappeared into the bathroom for a long time." This saddened them but it was late evening, and they had little choice but to go to bed.

In the morning, as per habit, they made their beds, left the bathroom neat and dry and offered to help with breakfast. Immediately, the attitude of their hosts changed! The hosts later told them that they had recently had a bad experience with a couple of guests who had left their house dirty and had not lifted a finger to help.

"Once their doubts were eased, we were really touched by their hospitality," remembers Kamla. "My brother had asked us simply to look them up but they insisted we stay with them, and so we did." The couple had packed some 50 *gur ki rotis* to last them through the trip, knowing that the food in Singapore would mostly be non-vegetarian. "Guess what—the family with whom we stayed also began eating what we cooked; they liked it so much!" she chuckles.

They grew so close that when the couple finally left, their hosts gifted Kamla a gold bangle. At the Delhi airport, her brother came to receive the couple and put them on the train to Ludhiana.

Soon after, they flew to London. Here too, they had family friends, and everyone had a good time.

A special visit to Kolkata is etched in Kasturi Lal's memory. One of his father-in-law's relatives, Shri Bansi Lal, lived there. "Our date of arrival and other details were duly sent to what was then Calcutta. Upon reaching there, we didn't realise that there was no such station as 'Calcutta' and that we were supposed to get off at Howrah! Initially, we were quite shocked to see the crowds and the grime of the station, but when we saw the magnificent Howrah Bridge, our spirits lifted.

"Somebody from Shri Bansi Lal's family had come to receive us. They lived in an area called Bhowanipore. Their house was big, but in dire need of repairs. However, they were not permitted to carry out any renovations by law. We stayed with them for five days, and had a super time—with lots of food, tea, conversation and card games.

"They took us to visit their shop in Bangdi Market. We were amused to note that the shopkeepers took off their shirts in the morning and spent the entire day sitting in their vests! We met some of our relatives in Bada Bazaar. They showed us around the city, and we particularly loved the museums and the aquarium."

And so it continued throughout their life. "My husband took me all over the world, just as I wanted to. I don't think he ever gave me a reason to complain. I feel very blessed," Kamla concludes, a happy smile playing on her face.

Kasturi Lal's eyes too light up at the memory of his numerous travels. Though the memories have faded with time, there are particular trips he remembers with fondness, and he recounts stray moments from his UK–USA trip with family.

"In 2012, I visited London with my wife to meet our granddaughter Vani, who was working after completing her studies. I was astonished and impressed to see how well she had adjusted to the tough life of a big city. The one week was beautiful. Afterwards, we travelled to Birmingham, where my old friend from Ludhiana, R.S. Sahdev, lives. It was wonderful to explore the city and its surroundings with him and his family.

"It was an extended trip, which took us to New York. As had been meticulously planned, my grandson Akhil, his wife Sumedha and my great granddaughter Bhavika met us at the London airport, and we flew to New York. The 10-day visit opened my eyes to the splendour of the world's most famous nation.

"New Jersey was next door to New York, and the revered saint Shri Sushil Kumarji had set up the famous Siddhachalam Teerth there. I am glad I was able to contribute a sum of one lakh to it, with my father's photograph placed there as my humble tribute.

"From New York we went to Niagara Falls, Buffalo City, then onward to Washington DC via Philadelphia. I remember being overwhelmed at the sight of the White House—such majestic grandeur!

"Our journey to the US ended in Miami, Florida, where we spent a good time with my daughter-in-law Sumedha's relatives Ashok and Kavita."

10

Yesterday, Today and Tomorrow
Insights on Life by Kasturi Lal Jain

"As a child in Kasur, I drank milk with ghee every single day. Why only me, everybody drank milk. Half a litre a day was the norm; in fact, it was almost a fashion to drink it. Anyone who could afford this rich treat was considered to be well-off. We had four buffaloes, which my father tended to. From the milk, butter would be churned, and from the butter, *lassi* would be derived—and that *lassi* was chock-full of health benefits. And despite the consumption of such rich dairy products, people were not fat. Today, the trend for people is to drink alcohol before sleeping—that's all I will say!"

"Toilets in many parts of India are still constructed 'Indian-style', which is the right posture to defecate in. Today, we have western commodes, which do not allow complete emptying of the bowels. Peoples' knees don't bend anyway."

"Until the 1950s and the 1960s, the word 'worry' was never used in our households. It was a carefree time. We worked hard, ate our meals together and slept peacefully. Walking to work and back, climbing stairs—these were things that one never even thought about; they were sort of 'automatic!'"

"In those days, words such as *mehnat* and *imandari* were taken for granted. I mean, they were a way of life. No one consciously thought 'I am hard-working' or 'I am honest'. We just did what we had to do. Whatever we earned was what our karma and our destiny had ordained for us, so words like 'jealousy', 'greed' and 'covetousness' were absent from our dictionaries. Today, I see dishonesty even among brothers. There is a lot of style and comfort in modern life, but 'peace' has gone missing…"

"Some of our extended family has its roots in Sialkot, Pakistan. I have seen times when up to 150 family members lived in the same house, and ate food made on one *chulha*. That is the extent of togetherness there used to be."

"I travelled for the first time to Ahmedabad in the 1950s. It was an eight-day stay, during which I did not eat a single meal in a hotel. I simply walked into shops owned by Jains, and after a brief conversation, an implicit understanding was established—both sides were good, honest and devoted to religion. And that was enough for them to offer me their hospitality. Today, people travel the world on business and stay in hotels."

"With prosperity comes sloth, and one just has to look around to realise that. I like the Japanese philosophy of life. They are hard-working as well as healthy. In their daily lives, they take no more than 20 minutes of rest. And they always leave 20% of their hunger unsatiated. There is no retirement, no craving for 'free time'. That is my kind of lifestyle. In our Jain community as well, we believe in eating only as much as required."

"In my time, eating a *chapati* was a soul-satisfying experience, because the *kanak* or wheat was pure and a high-energy food. Ladies would hand-pound all the spices in our households. I have grown up on pure food, and have no concept of eating heavy hotel food. If I am invited somewhere and only *chhole* have been cooked, I'll eat. But in my own home, food has to be light and simple."

"In the olden days, disease was not common. People usually died either of hunger or old age. Hardly anyone ever took medication."

"Whatever you do in this life, all the debit and credit, is carried forward in your future births. People say all your good and bad deeds are accounted for in this life itself. I don't think so. One lifetime is not sufficient for all the accounts to be settled. According to what you make of this life, you are reborn as a cow, buffalo, mosquito or worm. If you keep that in mind, it becomes easier to practice being good, which is the essence of religion."

SECTION TWO

THE FAMILY

Sunil Jain
Elder son

Born in 1955, Sunil Jain has dedicated more than 40 years of his life to the business. He started supporting his father at the age of 15 and, since then, has been a rock-solid pillar of the family. It is a testimony to the respect and trust he commands that the entire financial handling of the company is under his care.

His unassuming manner and candid reflections make Sunil Jain a wonderfully warm personality to interact with. Here is his take on the business and the family, with special focus on his relationship with his father:

"My father took me under his wing quite early in life. I was just a youngster when I stepped in to help my father, who was very active in his community. In 1971, I had joined college. Then in 1972, I got admission in Punjab Engineering College, which had only a 2% quota for non-residents of Chandigarh. But I saw the situation at home and realised I needed to be there for my father.

"In any case, children in those days did not study much. Most people would say, 'Ok, so this kid doesn't seem to be interested in studies… *isko dukaan pe bithaa do.*' So it was almost a given that I would join the family business at an early age.

"I travelled with my father quite extensively during the 1970s. Each trip was an immense learning experience, much richer than what I would have learned in a classroom. The amazing thing was, he would enter a prospective shop without hesitation. We still don't have that kind of confidence.

"His ability to make and maintain solid relationships is serving us to this day. All over India, he knows people of all hues. Even today, we find it difficult to build such close equations with others with such ease. It is truly a gift he has, and all we are doing is nurturing the relationships that he has already developed.

"In 1974, my father and his brothers formally separated. Conflicts had started brewing a couple of years before that, which isn't unusual; it is a common pattern in family businesses. The interesting thing is, brothers will first fight, then eventually agree to divide their shares amicably, because at the core of it all our values and feelings do come into play.

"Between 1970 and 1974, the business did suffer a lot. The interpersonal disagreements among the siblings resulted in low production, and therefore big losses. One by one, the brothers went their own way, and the process of dissolution began.

"My first advice to my father was to pay more attention to the business, rather than be too involved with the community. He agreed, and shifted his focus back to work. The business we are in required a lot of personal involvement. Back then, and even today in many parts of Punjab, it remains an unorganised sector. So we literally had to give it our sweat and tears. From making the products to packing and selling them, all of it required relentless effort.

"We have always been a simple family, so we never had to worry about putting food on the table, but it was emotionally quite stressful for us. Even so, my father remained cool and focussed on his work.

"My father commanded immense goodwill in the market, so we were able to source raw material without having to set down a collateral. This really helped us. In turn, my father was extremely particular about returning every single penny as soon as we sold our products. He made sure we did this on a daily basis. This solid business practice earned him even more respect and trust.

"At that time, we used to make only mufflers. Life and things were simple. There were no hassles of obtaining licences, and one made whatever one thought would sell. Slowly, we started making cardigans as well.

"Until today, my father is so deeply respected that no one in the family answers him back. His opinions are often a bit hard for us to understand. Maybe he says all the right things but we lack the experience and understanding. For example, he insists that we spend less, which per se is good advice based on his own experience. But in today's day and age, it is almost impossible to maintain a basic standard of living without spending.

"From 1974 to 1981, we worked day and night, starting our day at 7 a.m. and ending it past midnight. But still, we did not seem to earn much. It was quite puzzling. Slowly, we realised that one of our old, trusted employees was quietly siphoning off a lot of our stuff. In those days, people worked on trust. There was no stock audit. He took full advantage of that.

"His modus operandi was clever. We would ask him to open the shop on Sunday morning, which gave him the opportunity to smuggle out items that he had packed on Saturday evening itself.

"The first clue came when someone from our family went shopping for vegetables and remarked that the employee had been buying them at a much higher rate. Some days later, a neighbour asked us if we were giving this employee some stuff to take home. We were surprised and said of course not. 'Well, I saw him walking out with a big roll of green wool,' he told us.

"The following Monday, we checked and found that some of our rolls were missing indeed. We questioned him, and he began hedging. Of course, that had got the wind up him, and he never came back from home after lunch. Instead, he started telling everyone that we were maligning him instead of appreciating 30 years of his hard work. So I took a friend of mine and went up to his nephew, who was studying in school. The boy confessed that his uncle used to smuggle goods from our shop and hide them. He took us to the hiding place and we recovered a lot of our things.

"The next year, in 1982, we did a proper stock audit and realised that we had been losing up to 20% of profit. It was heart-breaking that all our labour had gone to waste all these years. The person was dismissed from our shop and our lives.

"On a positive note, the stock audit made us realise that we were doing well. We were very clear that all our incoming profits would be ploughed back into our business. Except for keeping money for our daily needs, we never used it for any indulgences. Our business did not require major investment at that time. Machines were cheap, and we were a hands-on family.

"In about 1977, my brother Bipan stepped in. He and I are different as chalk and cheese. He has always been a visionary and a forward thinker. He brought with him a freshness of ideas. He wanted to make fancy stuff, which we had never explored. Of course, we realised that the customers' tastes differed widely from state to state—my father mostly catered to clients from Gujarat, Rajasthan and Assam... and each region had its own demands.

"Bipan's ideas brought in a more stylish element to our products, with different colours and a touch of embroidery. My father was mostly supportive of his efforts, but he worried a lot about how to keep catering to his existing customers. He also wondered what sense it made to spend more on manufacturing and earn less profit. His points were valid, but of course we could have kept both streams running. It was a period when the older generation was struggling to understand the ideas of the new.

"Slowly, we continued to make mufflers but stopped the cardigans for the time being, to allow Bipan to follow his new trail of thinking. It worked well for us, and customers started asking for our new range of products. Bipan's vision helped us grow exponentially.

"The period from the 1980s to the 1990s saw a lot of innovation and growth in our company. Bipan introduced the Gold Queen label, which did well. We began supplying to two streams of wholesale markets—Sadar Bazaar and Gandhi Nagar in Delhi—as well as big retail stores.

"It was only a matter of time before we opened our first retail counter. And then there was no looking back. With the introduction of my son Akhil and then Vibhav into the business, there was even more growth and innovation. We managed to divide our responsibilities quite seamlessly, thanks to the immense love and understanding we share. My brother and children travel a lot, while I am happy to handle the financial affairs of the business.

"Every year, we share every detail of our earnings and losses with the family. It is extremely important to be transparent and honest, so that year-by-year, everybody knows where we stand and there are no misunderstandings. Until now, we have kept our responsibilities separate but maintain common accounts. However, we are practical enough to realise that things change and the world is changing at a fast pace. Our children have grown up; they have spouses, and tomorrow their children will also grow up and grow wings. We will, at some point, create a clear family charter so that there is no reason for conflict.

"No matter how far and wide we travel for studies or work, one thing is crystal clear among our family members—we do not smoke or drink. We do not gamble or indulge in carnal pleasures. In our times, it was a huge thing to sneak out from school to watch a movie. Today's youngsters—even adults— have a whole lot of options. But our moral grounding is so strong that common vices have failed to tempt us.

"When we went to drop my son Akhil to the NIFT in Delhi, my parents worried that he would fall into bad company, but I was sure he would be fine. And indeed, we need not have worried.

"We have consciously cultivated simplicity in our lifestyle. I used to make Akhil travel by bus to Delhi in peak summer to let him experience the hard life. It is essential for survival and a reality check. Even today, we live our lives without wanting to indulge in a display of material comforts; among the vehicles we own, most are workhorses that take us to our separate factories.

"It is also wonderful that we have very open channels of communication amongst ourselves. Our dining table is our meeting ground, where we discuss strategies, figure out ways to overcome hurdles and generally bond with each other.

"My father does keep pointing out that opting for funding is not a good idea. Being a traditional merchant, his firm opinion is that only money earned must be invested, rather than borrowed amounts. He is unhappy with the slightest delay in repaying loans, but then it does end up happening; things haven't exactly been hunky dory for business across the country in recent times.

"And then, we have a large ship, and it won't sail until it is adequately fuelled. This is one area where we sort of struggle to arrive on the same page. Of course, each of us has the same end goal; it is just a difference of approach."

Bipan Jain
Younger son

"I am five years younger than my brother, Sunil Jain. From the beginning, I was a sort of different drummer—I liked to dress well. By then, education standards in the country were improving. So initially, my father got me admission into the Kendriya Vidyalaya in Ludhiana, but his wish was to send me to a school where I would learn good English. Dehradun was considered. But then, the same year, a convent school run by Christian missionaries opened in our city, and plans of sending me to boarding school were cancelled.

"Saint Teresa's Convent began its innings in simple settings, with us students sitting under tents. But we were taught well, and from lower kindergarten to high school, it was my alma mater. Not once was my father worried about Christian values clashing with our own beliefs—his faith in our moral grounding was too strong for that.

"I enrolled into the Government College for Boys in 1977, but by now I had developed a keen interest in business affairs. We had seven lectures a day in college, of which I would attend six and then ask a friend to stand proxy for me. I would rush back to our factory and sit with the technician, keenly observing him at work. I was not interested in mufflers and cardigans. Maybe I was ahead of the times, but I wanted to delve into fashionable women's wear.

"Instead of getting upset with me for not focussing on college, my father gave me the freedom to explore my interest. I made several mistakes, but he never criticised me. I cannot remember a single time he stopped me from doing anything I wanted.

"In 1981, somehow I had the impulse to leave Ludhiana; I just didn't want to work here anymore. So, I went to Delhi. We had a small shop in Sadar Bazaar. I started a small factory there, on the second floor. I began making t-shirts, but after almost a year, a theft happened there. I closed the factory and tried running a shirts business in Gandhi Nagar, another large wholesale market in Delhi. But even that did not work out well, so I returned to Ludhiana. Back in my city, I again tried making men's t-shirts, but once again, my lack of experience forced me to pause and rethink.

"During that journey, my father used to take me along with him for muffler and cardigan bookings. We travelled together to metro cities like Mumbai and Ahmedabad. In those days, train journeys were gruellingly long, especially in the summer months. I remember travelling in the month of May in the three-tier sleeper class. It was insufferably hot but because it was a peak time for bookings, that was the only time we had to go. My father cheerfully made the best of those journeys. He would hang a wet towel on the window and slice fresh cucumbers and tomatoes to make sandwiches for us.

"Those trips taught me a great deal about how business should be conducted. I observed how strong my father's relations with his clients were. He commanded deep respect from them and was always welcome at somebody's home—we never once had to stay in a hotel. People loved him so much they would insist on hosting us.

"Our hosts were people of my father's age, all experienced and wise people. Staying with them taught me a lot; a stray phrase here, a nugget of wisdom there.

"The other marvellous thing I learned from my father was the art of negotiation. After work, he liked to go shopping for gifts to bring back home and for his factory staff. So we would visit Mohammad Ali Road, Abdul Rahman Street and Zaveri Bazaar. I was amazed at his bargaining skills! He would negotiate for the best price, relentlessly, but always did buy something or the other.

"He has always had such good taste. I remember he bought beautiful crockery for our home, which you won't find easily now. Even though I travel so much, I haven't seen anything so stunning.

"I remember clearly how Madame originated. In 1985 or so, we had made an exploratory business trip to London. Then, in 1989, my brother and I went to Hong Kong. It was a new country, and though we did ask around locally as to which markets to check out and where to stay, nobody guided us properly. So, we landed up there, booked ourselves into a guest house and walked down to the metro station. It was all quite alien to us, and we had no idea how to travel by the metro. We asked a Pakistani gentleman for guidance, and he gave us precise directions. That, quite literally, marked the start of our journey.

"From that year on, we started going at least three to four times a year to South East Asia, and began checking out garment-based enterprises. It was in Indonesia, around the year 1992, that the concept of Madame took shape in my mind. In 1993, we launched the brand with a clear focus—women's western wear.

"The name Madame came about quite by accident. In 1989, I had started a brand called Gold Queen, under which we made only winter wear. We had an agent who marketed our products all over the country, including Delhi, Punjab and Uttar Pradesh. Some four years into that business, a conflict of interest arose. To cut a long story short, we had some 15,000 to 20,000 items piled up in our warehouses, and we could not sell them. It was at that point that the agent suggested that we end our engagement with him.

"I searched and searched until I hit upon the name Madame. It clicked into place, and we took off all the Gold

Queen labels and replaced them with Madame. We began marketing it under that name, and it took off. A couple of years later, the marketing agent admitted that he repented his decision to part ways. He lost hold of Gold Queen, and we eventually put it in abeyance.

"Today, Madame makes women's fashion wear in every kind of fabric. We make gloves, stoles and scarves in-house and outsource accessories such as handbags and shoes.

"As far as my father's involvement with the business is concerned, he has always focussed only on the product he launched—mufflers. Until three to four years ago, he was quite actively involved, but as often happens in business families, points of view differ, and newer generations have new ways of functioning. Sometimes, it is difficult for the older generation to understand or agree with that newness, and they end up shaking their heads and saying, 'Alright then, do it your way.'

"Besides being unfailingly honest, my father has always been ambitious. And he has also sold his products on his own terms, backed by his confidence in the quality that he brings to the table. In his time, Jain Amar mufflers were top of the line. There were customers who would not settle for anything less.

"We started our first Madame store on the 23th of February, 2002. For a good 14 years or so, I handled the brand entirely, from sales to marketing to designing and everything in between, except finance. Then with the infusion of young blood—Akhil and Vibhav—I slowly withdrew, so that I could give them a chance to come forward and take things ahead.

"If I were to share my innermost feelings, I am very clear that elders should learn when to let go. Today, we are a joint family. Tomorrow, if we part ways, I would probably be the first to move away, because my larger interest is that the company and the brand should always remain alive and keep going strong. I've seen families where people fight over the ownership of a label and eventually nobody really takes care of it, letting it wilt away and die. I would never want that for Madame.

"At the moment, we have more than 150 shops and counting. We had to close some of our stores because they were not being managed properly and began running into losses. When you over expand, you sometimes fail to analyse things properly.

"My father is a visionary. He is very far-sighted, no doubt, and can foresee what might happen even a decade down the line. But sometimes, his ability to communicate things in a positive manner is a bit compromised—he can see the picture clearly but providing a solution affably is not really his cup of tea. That sometimes leads to disagreements on both sides, creating conflict.

"I have always had big dreams for Madame. I wanted the brand to comprise women's western wear, western wear for younger women, for the older segment, ethnic wear, Indo-western, accessories. Till 2012, we had absolutely no losses. I opened a studio in Barcelona and ran it for two years. We called the Spanish brand Kamla, after my mother's name Kamla.

"The first year it did not work out properly. It was on a contract so we could not close it either. We started another store in Spain, some 30 kilometres from Barcelona. I could blame myself for the closures... looking back, I think I should have studied the market more thoroughly and hired professionals rather than trying to manage everything myself.

"We called Spanish designers here in Ludhiana three or four times and they developed a range that would sell there. We also stopped shipping from India. Instead, our local partner procured garments from Paris and sold them in Barcelona. But somehow, the sales did not pick up. The realisation is that you need to sit on people's heads if you want them to bring in revenue. For similar reasons the six or seven stores that we had in Saudi Arabia also eventually had to be closed.

"To his credit, my father never criticised my venture adventures and did not castigate me for making such big mistakes.

"In 2016, we had an income tax search that pushed us back by two years, both mentally and financially. I do believe sometimes your astrological stars are not favourable. For example, in 1975–76, my father started selling shawls and gave them interesting names such as Hema Malini and Jaya Bhaduri. Customers lined up for these items, but suddenly after a few months, sales started to plummet. Yes, the stars don't always shine down on you.

"When my son came into the business, he wanted to try making men's garments. I gave him the go-ahead. We started a store here in Gurugram, and we realised that the name

Kamla would convey an Indian ethnic feel, which was not our profile, so we replaced the 'K' with a 'C' and the brand Camla was born."

Designed in Barcelona, Camla derives its inspiration from European art and culture. It caters to men of confidence and women of substance and is going strong.

"Mistakes are a part of personal and business growth. I always look at them as learning experiences. It has been an eventful but highly educative journey."

Meenu Jain
Daughter

The youngest of Kasturi Lal Jain's children, Meenu is 14 years younger than Sunil Jain and seven years younger than Bipan Jain. Her sprightly countenance and pleasant manner are testimony to having been surrounded by warmth and affection all her life.

"Oh yes, I was the most pampered child," she says, without hesitation. "Being the youngest had amazing advantages. If I was unwell, my father did not go to work! I loved to eat fruits for lunch, and if we fell short, he would go buy an armload of them for me. Small things that meant a lot and kept me in a cocoon of care all through childhood. Even today, he walks up to my place in the evenings, just to give me a box of *jalebis* or something that has been cooked at home.

"The greatest thing I have learned from my father is the art of building and maintaining relationships. I emphasise the word 'maintaining' because building them is the easy part—

most people don't do what it takes to nurture a relationship. My father has a natural affinity for bonding with and caring for people, and I learned that from him.

"Another wonderful trait he has is the spirit of giving without expecting anything in return. Be it the destitute, the sick or saints, he will step forward without hesitation to help out. In fact, he actively asks around if we know somebody who is in need, so that he can help. But even in giving, he has a principle: give only as much as the person needs, so that they value what they have received.

"Once, my son's friend's mother was seriously ill and required urgent surgery, and they had no funds. Hesitantly, I asked my father to help with some money, and he gave it to me, without questioning me even once. The lady has recovered fully and is a teacher in DAV School now.

"My father's regular visits to our Jain saints are an act of complete faith. He just goes and sits by their feet, learning and imbibing, rather than crying about unhappiness. He loves to gift them yoga mats and *asanas* for meditation.

"Every year, on the 1st of January, my father makes donations to at least a dozen charities, including People for Animals, Beauty without Cruelty, UNICEF and a number of local *gaushalas*.

"This dedication to social causes is no longer a passion for him, it is an ambition, and he would be happiest if we, his children, carried it forward for eternity. His advice to us is specific: whatever you earn each month, set aside some of it to give away to those in need.

"The one pillar on which my father's life stands is hard work. We have seen days of hard struggle, and equally, we have seen him emerge from them with the power of diligence. I am what I am today—an independent woman with a thriving business—because he and my entire family supported me through a rough phase and inspired me to stand on my own feet.

"I must credit my mother for being the glue that has held our family so close together. She has been my father's anchor in his toughest times. There was a period of seven to eight pretty bleak years, when business was slow. During that time, the guidance of her Guruji Maharaj, who is based in Meerut, and her own positive attitude kept my father going. Slowly, the tide turned and things began to look up. Her support during the adversity ensured that my father and mother were bonded in companionship forever.

"In my own case, they were always there by my side, without letting me become dependent on them. Our household has a fleet of cars, but during my days of struggle, my parents deliberately let me travel by auto, so that I could work my way back to independence. I am so grateful for that.

"Today, we have become an ancillary to the main company, and my team of workers supplies products to our own brand. I am so deeply involved in my work that it makes me feel immensely fulfilled.

"While we have been extremely fortunate to have my father as our guiding light, I feel he too has earned himself our immense respect and love. With age, he has grown a bit set in his ways, but of course he still commands our utmost respect. I sometimes do take a bit of liberty, though; after all, I am his youngest child."

Neelam Jain
Daughter-in-law

Neelam Jain is the bridge between the older generation and the youngsters of the family. Her solid, reliable presence is reassuring for them all, and in matters of religion as well as personal values, she is a great source of knowledge and inspiration.

So deep is her dedication to her faith that she will travel miles on rough roads, sit and eat in the humblest of places and walk barefoot in the cold to pay respects to her deities and saints.

Her own inspiration comes daily in the form of guidance and instruction from religious teachers, who gently show her the path to peace and harmony. For instance, each morning, a WhatsApp message informs her of one or a few items to give up for the day. It is an exercise in self-control, one that she cheerfully and dedicatedly follows.

Neelam, also called Dolly, arrived in Kasturi Lal Jain's family as Sunil's bride in the year 1981. At that time, the business was growing, no doubt, but every single penny that came into the house cost tremendous amounts of sweat and toil. "I remember how hard Daddy*ji* worked, much more

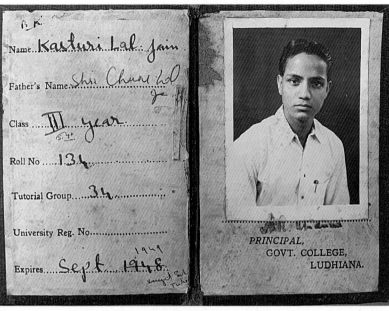

I-Card, Government College, Ludhiana, 1949

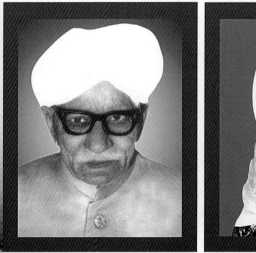

Father: Late Sh. Chunni Lal Duggar Jain;
Mother: Late Smt. Draupdi Devi Jain

Kasturi Lal Jain and Kamla Jain on their Engagement Day, 1952

A Recent Photograph of Kasturi Lal Jain and Kamla Jain

Kasturi Lal Jain, 1951

Kasturi Lal Jain: The Original Muffler Man

Third from Right: Pujya Puneet Muni Ji on Diksha Day;
Second from Right: Parashmal Ji Mandot; First from Right: Kasturi Lal
Jain; 1992, Mysore

Family Photograph of Four Generations, 2020

First Trip to North America with Grand-Daughter-in-Law
and Great-Grand-Daughter, 2012

At the All-India Franchisee Meet, 2016

Lifetime Achievement Award from Surya Dutta University, Pune, 2017

Kasturi Lal Jain at the Company's First Showroom

The Holy Pipal Tree, Where Jain Amar First Set Up Shop

Pujya Sumti Prakash Ji Maharaj

Paying Respects to Guru Maharaj in Maharashtra, 2019

than his sons even. They would go to bed at midnight, while he worked until 2.30 a.m. and sometimes beyond. I often wondered whether he got any sleep at all. At that time, our home was on the first floor and the factory was on the ground floor. He hardly ever came up."

She witnessed how one of the family's most trusted employees siphoned off their hard-earned money, without an ounce of scruples. "Daddy*ji* and the family trusted him so much that they even left the children in his care at night sometimes. He was never considered an outsider. But to do that to those who have such implicit faith in you… Life shows you strange things indeed."

This was exacerbated by the division of the family, which had happened just a few years before her marriage. Things were taking time to settle, and the resulting turmoil brought the family closer. "All the women of the house did their bit, both in running the home and business."

Neelam hails from Jammu and completed her studies there. When she first became a part of Kasturi Lal Jain's household, she would cover her head as a mark of respect for him. Then her brother-in-law Bipan got married, and Sangeeta Jain arrived into their family. Sangeeta was more "modern" in her approach and did not cover her head. Taking her cue from her, Neelam also stopped the practice, though her respect for her father-in-law remained intact and even deepened with time.

"Some years ago, when Daddy*ji* underwent knee surgery, I was constantly by his side. During that time, I opened up to him much more; the earlier formality and hesitation gave way to a comfortable bond," she shares.

"I take great inspiration from his spirit of generosity. I have seen first-hand how considerate he is. Some time back, two lady saints stayed with us for a few days. They were given a separate wing in the house. It was peak summer, brutally hot. The women saints do not use air conditioning. But my father-in-law made sure they were comfortable. When the ladies went out of their daily *gochari*, he would switch on the AC upstairs and turn it off before they returned. It was a touching gesture.

"Every single day, he wakes up with the thought of doing good and helping people. Be it bed sheets, blankets or *asanas* for mendicants, he is always thinking of producing and distributing these items to those in need.

"Of course, with age he has become a bit set in his ways. I've realised that he somehow expects us to understand his needs without having to articulate them, but of course, that is not always possible. That is usually the trigger for his outbursts. Sometimes, his candid comments tend to upset us, but he is the elder of our family, and our regard for him remains intact."

Akhil Jain
Eldest grandson

Born in 1982, Akhil is among the most vocal and dynamic members of the Jain family. After completing his studies from the National Institute of Fashion Technology (NIFT) Delhi, he joined the business in 2002. Today, he is one of the leading lights of the company, and he has achieved it through a combination of forward thinking and a result-oriented approach.

"It has been a phenomenal journey. But growing up, I was not close to my grandfather, and certainly not his favourite. He probably did not approve of certain things I did, and it made me feel he was not fond of me. But I have always been a realist and believe that, eventually, you are responsible for everything that happens to you. If he felt a certain way about me, it was my problem, not his."

In due time, Akhil managed to understand what had caused the initial hiccups in their relationship.

"I guess it has to do with the bloodline. We are all very straightforward and like to speak our mind. So my being similar to *Dadaji* in that sense probably created a sense of conflict between us.

"I was young and sensitive. Those days of adolescence are a period when everything hits you with twice the required force. So, I found myself reacting aggressively to trivial matters— why wasn't my opinion taken, why couldn't I have done this or that..."

Refreshingly honest in his self-assessment, he continues, "I have to admit I was arrogant and high-headed in my youth. For example, I would walk all the way from the Delhi railway station to Sadar Bazaar, refusing to sit in a rickshaw because it was below my dignity.

"It was my tenure in Delhi and my education at NIFT that brought about subtle changes in me. A big city teaches you to rough it out and become independent. Here I was, taking DTC buses, which are a perfect vehicle for bringing you to ground reality! When I went back to Ludhiana after my first stint in Delhi, everybody in the family noticed a massive change in my behaviour.

"Gradually, my relationships with them began to improve. I had not been close to my mother and my grandfather. But the new, somewhat reformed me grew steadily more likeable and accepted. I must give immense credit to my parents for their patience in dealing with me. I was not an easy child— quite a rebel, in fact. They could have thrashed me and punished me. Instead, they treated me with utmost care and understanding—that has always been an inspiration to my own self.

"I was not religious at all. But growing up, my mind absorbed everything like a sponge. I've always had a very scientific approach to life, and religion intrigued me for sure. It was one subject on which I bonded closely with my *Dadaji*. We spent countless evenings after dinner on the terrace, discussing religion and philosophy. For example, science has a different way of describing the sun and the moon, while our religious scriptures give us a totally different perspective. *Which is true? Why? How do we know?* I had endless questions, and my grandfather had endless patience. Besides, he was deeply knowledgeable—to my mind, he was the most learned person I knew. And he always had the time to talk to me, unlike my parents, who were engaged heart and soul in the affairs of the company as well as running the house.

"My grandfather has an unerring instinct for assessing people. He has the ability and the experience to judge how a person will turn out to be even 10 years from today. And for a business family, that is a huge gift. So, to this date, if I have to hire a senior person, I let him spend some time with the person. If his verdict is that the person does not seem reliable, and I do end up hiring him, he will be proved right within a short time—so powerful is the combination of his experience and instinct.

"I have learned all my basic skills and values from the elders in my family. From my grandfather, the importance of hard work and the ability to gauge people; from my uncle Bipan Jain, the quality of aggressive approach and innovative thinking; from my father, the art of giving without expecting anything in return.

"There have been times when I met an old acquaintance of the family, and the person told me how my father had lent him Rs 15,000 in his time of need, and how that amount helped him tide over a difficult situation. Not only that, my father assured him that it was okay to return the money when he could afford it. This is how my grandfather is too, so his generosity has rubbed off on my father.

"My grandfather has always had a very minimalistic and realistic approach to business. He hates wastage of any kind, and it upsets him to see even a random exhaust fan running needlessly in a small bathroom in the factory. Now our logic is that the bathroom is constantly in use by up to 50 people, so switching the fan off and on each time is a waste of time. But then that's the difference of both perception and approach that marks one generation from the other.

"Another sound advice he has for us is to study the market, study competition, study business models… not rush into things. This is always at the back of my mind, and I intend to devote more time to it.

"In our family, we are fortunate to have a combination of personality types. Ambitious, aggressive, patient, diligent… so we balance each other out, which is a big blessing. If I had to analyse, I would say I am quite similar to my uncle Bipan Jain, who has always been forward thinking, innovative and a little impatient.

"Because I study religion and introspect a lot, I am also constantly aware of the impermanence of things. Jainism teaches you to keep things in perspective. I am also very aware that my family has begun to rely on me and put me on a sort of pedestal, perhaps because I have stepped ahead and taken charge of moving things forward at a quicker pace. But because I am aware of it, I am also taking steps to ensure that this regard and respect does not turn sour in the years to come.

"During my journey with the company, I have seen a whole see-saw of ups and downs. The years from 2016 to 2019 were particularly odd, I would say. Odd in the sense I had never faced a scenario when our vendors or agents had to ask us for pending dues. We had always been able to keep our accounts clear, and whatever credit we took was given in good faith, based on years of painstakingly built relationships.

"However, life as an entrepreneur teaches you so much! Looking back, I think we over expanded during those years. And as a family, we have always believed that mistakes and setbacks are opportunities to grow, so they are beautiful in their own way."

Akhil has complete clarity on his plans for the future. "I would like to take myself off the business scene when I turn 55 and turn my attention to giving back to society. Of course, I am aware that I need to earn enough so that I can give generously. Jain kings and monarchs were all *chakravarti* rajas who gave up immense wealth. You cannot borrow to give.

"My core belief is that discipline is the key to growth, and following a regular rhythm in daily life as well as an organised schedule at work has allowed us to combine professional success with personal harmony. I am grateful for it all."

Sangeeta Jain
Daughter-in-law
Wife of Bipan Jain

Soft-spoken and slender, Sangeeta is a woman of few words but great substance. She hails from Delhi, where she did her graduation in commerce. Ever since her entry into Kasturi Lal Jain's family, she has been the rock-solid pillar behind her visionary husband.

"I married Bipan in 1985. My father owned a shop in Delhi's Sadar Bazaar and bought mufflers on wholesale from my future father-in-law. We did not know it then, but my mother and my mother-in-law's sister were good friends, who got to know each other because they often visited the same Jain Sthanak. At some point, they got talking, and the alliance was suggested.

"From the day I walked into the household, I was greeted with a refreshing openness from my parents-in-law. Despite their own traditional backgrounds, they never tried to rein me in. In fact, they encouraged us to go out and enjoy ourselves, ignoring our protests that we did not want to leave them alone.

"I was amazed to see how disciplined and hard-working Daddy*ji* was. Even today, he is sprightly and self-reliant to the extent that his health permits him. For us, his punctuality and sense of integrity were always a source of inspiration, and remain so.

"For a brief while, I did participate in the family business. We had launched an accessories brand called NYCiti, and for a few months I handled it. But then my children were studying and the new wing of our house was coming up, so I decided to step back for a while. At some point, I might consider taking up some aspect of the business, but for now I am content to be a source of support to my family.

"My personal passion is health, which I study in depth. Particularly healthy eating is something I both enjoy and try to inculcate among my family members. It's another matter that my father-in-law flatly refuses to try any of my 'healthy eats' saying they might make him sick! He likes his typical *desi* meal; nothing else will do.

"Age has made Daddy*ji* a bit short-tempered and impatient, but that is for us to understand and accept. The unwritten rule in our family is to accord our elders the utmost respect, and we live by that."

Vibhav Jain
Grandson

A man of few words, Vibhav has his path clearly charted out. The younger son of Kasturi Lal Jain's elder son Sunil Jain and brother of Akhil Jain, he was born in 1984. For someone still quite young, he displays an impressive understanding of the business and of life itself.

"I look after the production for all our brands. For Madame, I also handle some of the R&D. Soon after completing school in 2000, I headed to Germany and Japan for technical training.

"When I started working in the company, none of us had an idea that it would reach these heights. We used to sit in a small unit, make enough products to be able to sell them, and that was pretty much it. But the kind of experiences I have gained in the last two decades or so have been invaluable. The many mistakes we make teach us to self-correct and we as a family are never hesitant to acknowledge this fact.

"Some years ago, we had a short-circuit fire in the factory. It was a Sunday afternoon, which turned out to be a blessing in disguise. Because it was winter, traffic was low and the fire brigade arrived promptly, so a lot of damage was controlled. That was a lesson well learned, and we immediately put in precautionary measures to prevent another such episode.

"Although I do not interact much with my grandfather business-wise, his experience and wisdom in such matters are always with us. He advises us on how to structure our facilities so that we can segregate each unit and minimise damage in case another mishap strikes.

"We have a very open culture of communication in our family. Each of us has his separate responsibilities, but every evening, we sit around the dining table and have a free conversation about work. There is one unwritten rule— no matter how uncomfortable a situation or how wrong a decision, we have to tell the truth. This helps the business in the long run, because eventually hiding a mistake is only going to hurt us all.

"My grandfather has a very interesting piece of advice on how to balance work and home. He points out that work takes up most of our days and our lives and, in the process, we should not miss out on the companionship of our partners. He himself led a very busy life, so he used to take his wife along on many of his travels. So he encourages us to take our spouses along whenever we go out of town, and we try to do that as much as possible.

"As my elder brother, Akhil wants me to step up and be more 'visible', and that is such a great thing in today's world, where people tend to pull each other down. But I am happy doing my production work. I like to stay behind the scenes and am not very comfortable taking up responsibilities such as PR and marketing.

"Summing up, I would say we have been fortunate to be able to lead life the way we like, despite living in a joint family. Respect for elders and for others' feelings are inbuilt in us, so we seamlessly avoid conflict. For example, we have never had any restrictions on what we wear inside or outside the house. Even my grandfather cheerfully wore a pair of jeans when he travelled to America!

"The relationships he has built are incredibly strong. And that has helped the entire family as well as our business. It has also infused a culture of being socially bonded with the community. I think that is a great legacy that my grandfather has created for us to follow."

Vani Jain
Granddaughter

Attractive and articulate, Vani is the daughter of Bipan and Sangeeta Jain. Having studied outside Ludhiana for a good part of her life, she has spent perhaps the least amount of time with her grandfather. Even so, her admiration for Kasturi Lal Jain's values and wisdom is evident in her impressions of him.

"I went to the Convent of Jesus & Mary, Waverley, Mussoorie, at the age of 10. I completed my schooling there and did my graduation in Mathematics Honours at Miranda

House in Delhi. After passing out from college in 2008, I spent close to a year in Ludhiana—the reason being simply that I was waiting to join Infosys, where I had been selected for a job. That was an year of recession, so the joining date kept getting pushed, and after six months had elapsed, I decided not to take it up at all.

"My next destination was Nottingham, UK, where I studied Operations Management. Soon after, I landed a job as a data analyst in London, where I worked until 2017. Whatever time I have spent with my family in Ludhiana has been since that year. That is when I got the opportunity to interact with and get to know my grandfather. I soon realised that despite being two generations senior to us, he possesses an incredibly progressive and practical mind.

"It is wonderful to see how he consciously tries to bridge the gap between old and new, traditional and modern, without being too judgmental. I also admire the way he has retained his zest for work. To see him still going to the factory and finding new things to do is inspiring for us all. For example, the *asanas* he makes for monks to sit and meditate on were entirely his idea—he turned leftover fabric into a great product! Not only that, he decided to print spiritual quotations on the *asanas*, another one of his unique ideas. The great thing is that the *asanas* are not just decorative items. They have immense utility for those who practise meditation; I have seen people asking for more.

"Another great trait in my grandfather is his attention to detail. Even now, the smallest of imperfections rarely escapes his attention. Age has done little to diminish his inquisitive nature, and I find it refreshing that he is eager to make friends with new technology. If there is a new phone or app, he wants to learn it rather than resist it. And he is a keen learner, too.

"I recently got married, and it struck me as to how practical and supportive of my wishes my grandfather was—which is remarkable considering how traditional his own background has been. He assured me that I did not have to marry for the sake of 'settling' and that I had his support in whatever decision I would take. This helped take the pressure off my mind tremendously, and I consider it a huge blessing.

"For the past couple of years, I have seen up close how social and generous he is, always ready to help those in need. At some point in my life, I would like to emulate his values and perhaps join an NGO."

Sumedha Jain
Granddaughter-in-law of Kasturi Lal Jain
Wife of Akhil Jain

A beautiful young mother of two, Sumedha did her schooling from Bal Bharti School in Delhi, followed by a Bachelor's in Fine Arts from Amity University, Noida. But while she was in the second year, a marriage proposal came, and soon, she took her vows with Akhil Jain.

"When the time came for my husband Akhil to get married, he told his grandfather, 'I will not choose a life partner for myself. Whoever you deem fit to be my wife, I will accept.' That is how much respect and faith he has for his *Dadaji*. In this day and age, it is rare for someone to take this traditional approach to marriage, but Akhil knew that his grandfather has an unerring instinct for judging a person's character and strength of mind."

Pausing, she reflects on the 14 years gone by, and chuckles. "Try convincing today's generation to leave the decision of their marriage to their elders! You will straightaway be told that those times are gone; this is the modern age. Why look far? Even in our own family, youngsters have a very independent mind-set.

"We avidly believe in horoscopes, so the first step to our marriage was the matching of our *kundalis*. Once they were found to be compatible, my grandfather-in-law, grandmother-in-law and mother-in-law came over to meet me. I am from Delhi, but my mother is from Ludhiana. Her side of the family knew Akhil's family very well, even back in those days when they lived in Wait Gunj.

"I had, until then, not thought either this way or that about marriage, so I had no objection to the match. It was destiny, and it brought us where we are today. Until today, *Dadaji* proudly claims that he is the one who got me into the family.

"Speaking of *Dadaji*, he is the elder of our family. In every person, there is much good and some weaknesses, but from day one, I have maintained that he is the patriarch of the family, and we all have to accord him due respect and love. We all try to adopt and follow everything that is good about him, and he has a lot of good in him."

The impression that emerges from Sumedha's account of Kasturi Lal Jain is this: he is a man of intense discipline. At times, this might translate into a certain rigidity of approach, which is not always understood or liked by the younger members of the family. But one remarkable quality he has is his ability to take the right decisions.

"We have realised this time and again," says Sumedha. "At a certain moment, when he asks us not to take a certain decision, however big or small, we do tend not to agree with his views. But almost always, we later find that his advice was correct. He has that inner strength of character, which makes him sift the grain from the chaff and see things for what they are."

Even today, Kasturi Lal Jain is active in the family business, though of course age and health do not permit him to be involved full-time. When the original Jain family separated, Kasturi Lal Jain's company continued to be called Jain Amar, while other brothers tweaked the business name to Jain Amber and such.

Sumedha shares a bond of respect and affection with her grandfather-in-law. "*Dadaji* often shares stories from his life with us. And it is heart-wrenching to hear about the lean times the family went through. Things used to be so difficult that they sometimes lived on just flour and milk, kneading their *rotis* either with salt and chillies or sugar. Of course, milk yielded all the high-protein dietary requirements such as yogurt and butter. Vegetables were a luxury that they could not afford regularly. Even during Diwali, there was sometimes not enough to buy even *diyas*…"

"*Dadaji* also narrates how, in spite of the penury, his mother would always make extra *rotis* to feed the hungry and the stray dogs and cattle in the neighbourhood. He would address his mother as *Bhabhiji* and his father as *Baiyaji*. In those times, many people would not address their parents as *Ma* and *Pitaji*."

"Even today, he wakes up and decorates the little temple in the house. He wakes up around 4 a.m., at the crack of dawn, has his bath and decorates his personal temple. Then he does his meditation and prayers, followed by a short nap. Around 8 a.m., he takes a breakfast of milk—he is a big lover of milk, and he needs to have it with full cream. We get fresh dairy milk, and it is unthinkable for *Dadaji* to go without his glass of warm milk either in the morning or evening. He takes almonds and *murabba* along with the milk. Then every two hours, something light, such as fruit.

"We as a family are lovers of sweets, so that is one thing he cannot resist. *Choori*—roti crumbled with ghee and sugar—is one of his favourites. Sometimes he has just that as his entire dinner. In winter, he must have his *bajra* and *makki ki roti* with *shakkar, pinni, shakkarpara*… typical village food. That is his taste. He likes our *Dadiji* to make these things for him with her own hands.

"One thing about *Dadaji* is that he is very self-dependent. For example, he will never tell us he is not feeling well. Instead, he will just keep sleeping till late. Sometimes, it becomes difficult for the family to realise there is something up with his health, because we are all busy with our lives and kids. In a childlike way, he tends to get upset that nobody noticed he was out of sorts. Then he has to be explained to that it is better to let the household know.

"Similarly, he has been advised to use a walking stick, but he refuses to use it. He will often take it with him to the car, but once out, he will never use it—in his mind, walking with a stick is a sign of dependence.

"He also hates having to hold someone's hand. Whether we are at the doctor's or at a function, unless there is a precarious step to climb, he will walk on his own, warning us with his eyes to let him keep going. That is the spirit he has always had, which makes us look up to him even more.

"Work has always been his life. Sometimes, he will go to the factory at 11 a.m., sometimes after lunch. Not that he can do much now, but just the feeling of going to work makes him feel productive, and that is very important for him. During the COVID-19 lockdown, it was very hard for us to convince him to sit at home.

"Apart from the factory, *Dadaji* has his own daily outings for charity. He does not like to talk about this, but we know that he likes to go out and buy ice creams and peanuts for the needy. He will take rounds of temples or go sit with a saint. He has his permanent driver and car, and he is his own master.

"In our family, we consider feeding a cow to be very auspicious. The fodder is called *patthe*, and *Dadaji* likes to go down to the local *gaushala* to feed the cows.

"Every single year, he finds new and creative uses for scraps of fabric and rejected material. He is full of ideas! All over India, he makes and sends beautiful repurposed *asanas* for *pooja*. The concept and design for these is entirely his, complete with the Jain Amar logo and even *mantras* printed on the *asanas*. Countless saints all across India have received them, thanks to *Dadaji*.

"Speaking of gifting, he also likes to personally visit and carry gifts for our extended family, which is huge. In Ludhiana alone, our *shareeka* of four generations comprises more than 40 families. *Dadaji* quietly and regularly pays them visits, maintaining relations and keeping the bond strong. Only his driver is privy to most of these activities; he does not like to talk much about his charitable acts.

"*Dadaji's* firm belief is that gifts must be given only to those who will actually value them, not to those who already have everything. Another of his strong beliefs is the practice of minimalism and simplicity. For example, his own room in the house marks a stark contrast to the rest of the bungalow. He keeps it simple. Whether it is a coat of paint or a new bed, he generally refuses to update or upgrade things just because he can—his life has always been an example of simple living and high thinking.

"We have learned so much from him, and we continue to benefit from his wisdom. The values of a family are drawn from its elders, and we have been very fortunate to have him as our guiding light."

Neha Jain
Granddaughter-in-law

Neha is the mother of twin boys—Sial and Sijans. She studied in Jammu at Presentation Convent. She did her graduation as well as post-graduation from Jammu and worked for nine months with HDFC. Throughout a gold medallist, she is grateful for having married into a family that values her qualifications and encourages her to put her education to good use.

Neha became part of Kasturi Lal Jain's family in 2010, when she married his grandson Vibhav. Her first impression of her future grandfather-in-law left an indelible stamp on her heart. "I had come down from Jammu to Ludhiana to meet Vibhav. It was our first meeting. We were served lunch, and I was stunned to see that Daddyji was serving each one of us with his own hands. By then, the family was a name to reckon with, and that is why his simplicity was so touching.

"Even after marriage, I never felt a generation gap with him. He is very open-minded, probably because he is so well-travelled. Whether we wear denims or shorts, he has never raised an eyebrow.

"Of course, he is very proper when it comes to his food. Although his meals are simple—*dal*, *phulka*, *subzi* and *makki ki roti, choori* in winter—he is particular that his daughters-in-law should serve him, properly in a plate. We also make sure that one of us is there for him. It is a small and simple thing, so we also do it with our heart.

"He is extremely fond of travelling. At night, we all sit in his room as a full family. In general, we talk about business or family. It is such a beautiful family that I have always felt very comfortable and loved. All our wishes and demands, said or unsaid, are fulfilled. I feel blessed.

"I have majored in Finance, but right now I am not working. My grandfather-in-law does encourage me to make full use of my potential, and at some point, I intend to do that.

"Daddy*ji* goes to the factory every day around 11 a.m. He likes to stay active. If not the factory, he goes and visits saints, never telling anyone about his many charitable activities.

"In everyday life, he is so positive in his approach. Even if one is in a negative state of mind, he will give one a new perspective. His dedication to religion is inspiring. Though I am a Jain by birth, I used to worship Lord Krishna. At my paternal home, I kept Lord Shiva's fast for eight to nine years. I would never listen to the *pravachans* of Jain saints. I gravitated towards Lord Krishna for some reason. When I arrived into this household, they never forced me to embrace their own faith, but watching the entire family had a great influence on me.

"I have learned to be an optimist. I used to be a pessimist. I have learned to believe in goodness. I have seen how grounded they are, and it has impacted me.

"When I met Vibhav for the first time, his attitude towards waiters, drivers and cooks made a great impression on me. He was incredibly polite and nice to them all. I think more than anything else, that helped me make up my mind; a person and family who respect those who are less privileged have to be good-hearted.

"Before marriage I used to travel in comfort. Now, we stay in *dharamshalas* all across India. My father-in-law once took us to Badrinath–Kedarnath, where we stayed in very basic hotels. My in-laws taught me to adjust to any situation. Even during our honeymoon, we stopped over at Bangalore on our way back from the Maldives. We were about to book a hotel, but one of Daddy*ji*'s acquaintances insisted we stay with them. It was a very basic place, but we spent three nights with them, and their family's warmth touched us to the core.

"In fact, sometimes we wonder how we will be able to keep alive all the wonderful relationships that he has weaved across the country. I hope we can!"

Ashish Jain
Grandson

Young and dynamic, Ashish brings with him the confidence and freshness of modern times. He is handling the company's Camla brand, from R&D to accounts and everything in between. An undergraduate in business management from

Durham University in England, he graduated in 2013 and joined the family business soon after.

"Camla was the brainchild of my father Bipan Jain. It was a joint venture with a Spanish concern, born out of our desire to start operations in Europe. Soon, we thought of introducing it in India as a fashion brand with a western touch. It was a good time to do that, since many international brands were coming into India at that point. The name conveyed a contemporary vibe and worked well for us because it is derived from my *dadi's* name. I stepped in at the point when we decided to launch it here in India, around 2014–15.

"When we started, the brand had only women's clothing, but I added a men's range to it. So now we have both. Its USP is fast fashion catering to premium customers. Though we have a team of in-house designers, I am actively involved in designing clothes for Camla.

"I've spent nearly a decade outside Ludhiana, so frankly I haven't had the opportunity to get really close to my grandfather, but his very presence in our life is a great source of inspiration as well as guidance. He is a self-made man who has for the longest time resisted carrying a stick to walk around with. By the same logic, he detests bank loans and tends to be risk-averse. I see where he is coming from but, at the same time, growing a fashion brand in the modern scenario does require you to take some risks.

"My relationship with *Dadu* is sweet, quite literally. My mother is very health-conscious, so our family usually gets to eat only the 'healthy' stuff. From time to time, my grandpa sends across a small box of sweets, which he knows I love. It is a beautiful gesture, and I always value it.

"When I returned from London, I was impressed by how much in sync with the times grandpa was. He has always had a progressive approach to life and understands that things change with the passage of time. So his reaction to my way of dressing and thinking was pleasantly positive. The only advice he gave me was to cut down on partying with friends and focus on the business. When I began doing that, I realised how right he was—running an enterprise takes everything out of you. It is energy-intensive and requires all your attention. I am grateful for that."

Going forward, Ashish is open to doing a short-term technical course that would help him bring more ideas to the business. He has big ambitions for Camla and admits he is constantly thinking ahead, while also reminding himself that he must keep the bigger picture in mind. After all, Jain Amar is where it all started, and it is under that umbrella that they have all grown.

SECTION THREE

A CLOSE CIRCLE OF FRIENDS

Subhash Kankariya
Friend

Warm and amicable, Subhash Kankariya has been a close family friend of the Jains for close to three decades now.

"I was born in 1956 in Pune and have lived all my life in this city. I got to know Kasturi Lal *ji* in the year 1994, when he came here, possibly for a community event—it is a bit too far back in time for me to remember our first meeting. But we grew really close only in the year 1998, when we attended a *pravachan* of Muni Sumti Prakash *ji*. It was the *chaturmas* period—four months during which the gurus remain where they are. For their followers, it is a golden opportunity to meet and learn from them.

"I have always known Kasturi Lal Jain to be a wonderfully social, amicable person. He is always ready to lend a helping hand to those in need. His contribution to the Jain community is immense. Their welfare is always on his mind. Thoughtful gestures like making woollens and *asanas* for them are par for the course for him.

"Though he is quite a few years my senior, our bond is one of deep friendship. Even if I sometimes delay in connecting with him, he makes sure he stays in touch. We stay in each other's homes whenever we travel to Pune or Ludhiana, and our families too are equally close."

Ramesh Malhotra
Family astrologer

Gentle and mild-mannered, Ramesh Malhotra brings in a sense of serenity with his sheer presence. His unruffled manner and experienced eyes tell you that this is a man who has not only seen the world but understood that there is a power above that guides people and their destinies. Perhaps it is this knowledge that explains his wise vibe.

"Your affinity towards a certain discipline is often carried over from your last birth," he reflects. He displayed an interest in palmistry when he was just four years old. By the time he was in Class X, astrology had him hooked, and he began studying it intensely.

Malhotra met Kasturi Lal Jain's son Sunil at the Government College in Ludhiana, where they were both students. Their friendship grew, and soon, he happened to meet Kasturi Lal Jain too.

"When I met Jain *saab* for the first time, he seemed a bit disenchanted—some fake astrologers had deceived him. It was his wife who gently persuaded him to hear me out. I did not say much, except that I could foresee some trouble with a government-related issue in his life. He did not respond, and left."

Soon, the astrological predictions came true. There arose a dispute at his Dana Mandi property, and he was quite troubled. Just a few days later, he walked up to Malhotra's place and that is when a lifelong relationship of trust began. This was the year 1974.

"Today, the Jain family consults me on everything from births to occasions and business matters. In the nearly five decades that I have known him, Kasturi Lal Jain has never once veered from his principles. He is one of the most generous men I have known. Once he has given you his word, he will never break it, come what may. And when it comes to hard work, there is simply no compromising in his book. This *karmath* nature runs in their genes—both his sons are extremely diligent.

"I call him a 'yug purush', whose blessings mean the world to us."

Dr. Ram Pal Jain
Family physician

The gentle Dr. Jain, a general physician, has known the Jain family since 1974. Since then, he has not only treated them but also forged an unshakeable bond with each member of the family.

"I cannot remember the first time I met Kasturi Lal Jain—it was just seamless, also because we both belong to the Jain *samaj*. I have seen him work endless hours, right from the days when the business was in its infancy. Very few men I have met are as religious and as diligent as him.

"In his life, he has worked hard for everything he has achieved. For two to three months, he would not sleep, returning late in the night and waking up at 3 a.m. even in winter. After a bath and meditation, he would be off to work once again. Of course, as his physician, I would gently advise him to take it easy, but he always said, 'Nothing will happen to me.' And fortunately, nothing did. Hard work runs in this family's genes.

"I have personally witnessed their rise from one small shop to all these factories and showrooms. There was a time in the 1970s when Kasturi Lal made only mufflers. The yarn was pure wool, wonderfully warm. I remember buying three mufflers for Rs 51, at Rs 17 a piece. Jain Amar has always been a company with a fantastic reputation, built on solid quality.

"Kasturi Lal revered his parents and served them with all his heart. Their concern for each other was very touching. In those days, we did not have cars and scooters, so father and son would walk down to check on each other. They always insisted on paying me my fee, even if it was 5 rupees. In matters such as these, they are extremely particular.

"Until today, if Kasturi Lal has to pay Rs 51 to somebody, he will pay the Re 1 first and the remaining Rs 50 later. His logic is simple: 'If I can afford to pay Rs 50, why can't I pay Rs 51?' This value-based business ethic has filtered down to his family, and that is the secret of their immense success. I have seen big family businesses crumble because the children were not competent or honest enough. The Jains will always be trusted and prosperous because they have their core principles right."

SECTION FOUR

THE OLD FAITHFULS

SCORES of employees at the Jain household and company have been with them for two decades or more. That in itself is a strong validation of the family's values. Even a quick conversation with these men and women reveals the love and respect they have for its patriarch—Kasturi Lal Jain. Having been a vital part of and witness to his phenomenal journey, they have seen first-hand how he rose from *farsh* to *arsh* (ground to sky) by dint of his diligence.

Here are some snippets from their recollections and opinions:

Satish Kumar Rajput
Sales and Marketing

Rajput joined Jain Amar in 1986, after a rather thorough personal interview.

Back then, his duties involved cutting threads and packing the finished products. There was only one factory, in Sunder Nagar. Work used to continue till late in the evening inside one big hall; in the morning, the goods would be sent to the shop. Even in those early days, Jain Amar used to churn out nearly 10,000 mufflers. They also made blouses and cardigans for women and pullovers for men.

Rajput has seen the company through huge ups and downs and learned both skills and life lessons with each trough and crest. "Working with *Bauji* has been the most wonderful experience of my life," he says. "When I came, I was very young, and knew next to nothing about the business. It was *Bauji*'s patient guidance that taught me how to conduct myself and deal with other clients."

Combined with days and years of endless hard work, the training paid off, and today he handles a major set of responsibilities for the enterprise with great confidence. "There were times when we worked three continuous nights but never complained because the owners themselves were so dedicated," he recalls.

From 1986 to 1993, the work hours were gruelling, and the family plunged themselves into labour without considering day or night. "From Tuesday to Thursday, we worked almost non-stop," recalls Rajput. "Saturday, the products would reach the shop." By then, they were also supplying wholesale Jain Amar stocks to Bangalore, but there were a couple of hard years when sales were quite low.

Then came Madame, and the company's fortunes began to pick up. For Rajput, each phase of the company's growth has added valuable personal wisdom. "With Kasturi Lal *Bauji*, our focus was completely on wholesale, which involved tremendous amounts of hard work and discipline. With the advent of Madame, the importance of brand building dawned on us. And each new generation brought with it a new wave of ideas and innovation. We've moved towards IT and automation, thanks to Akhil Jain. I enjoy this!"

Suresh Kumar Rana
Joined Jain Amar in 2000

There is a reverence in Suresh Rana's voice as he talks about *Bade Babuji*. Rana comes from a defence background, where nearly all of his close relatives are in the Navy or Air Force. "I was the only one who chose this profession, and I have never regretted it," he says.

Since Rana joined Jain Amar in 2000, *Bade Babuji* has been like a father figure to him. Step by baby step, he taught the newcomer how to handle factory workers, how to conduct himself and how to ensure discipline.

"And he always led by example," shares Rana. "Since the day I joined, and until very recently, *Bauji* would come to the factory at 8 a.m., come rain or shine. And he would leave only after making sure that the last employee had exited the premises. Safety and welfare have always been topmost in his mind where we are concerned."

The most valuable lesson Rana learned from *Bauji* was the art of handling people. "He has a great instinct for assessing a person—with the lethargic, he is strict, and with the diligent, he is lenient. These are things I have imbibed from him over the decades.

"After creating and leading the enterprise from the front for more than half a century, *Bauji* has devoted himself to creating gifts for the saints he reveres. From leftover scraps of material, he designs *asanas* so that the mendicants can sit in comfort. His days are spent donating as much as he can, doing as much good as he can."

No wonder, then, that workers like Rana have never left. In fact, from the way Rana speaks about the company and its fortunes, it is evident that there is a deep sense of belonging.

Joginder Nath
Cashier

Joginder joined the Jains in 1995. He started working as a thread marker, moved on to tailoring and then got promoted to the post of Cashier at the Noorwala factory.

"All that I have earned and learned, I owe to *Bade Bauji*," he begins. "I completed my 11th standard in 1958 and started working soon after. When I began, I was a complete novice. Bauji mentored me painstakingly, and he soon saw that I was a good worker. He knows how to value those who are diligent, so he started giving me more responsibilities. The wonderful thing is that he treated all his workers as part of a big family, not as employees.

"I have always admired his keen attention to detail. Nothing escapes his experienced eye; not even the smallest glitch in a stitch. In the early days that I worked with him, he would arrive at the factory at 7 a.m. sharp and get ready to let in the workers at 9 a.m. His dedication to work, his punctuality and discipline have filtered down to each member of his family.

"For the past few years, I have not worked closely with Kasturi Lal *Bauji*, but working with his sons and grandsons is equally rewarding. The only big difference in the working styles of the three generations is the advent of computers and technology. But when it comes to hard work, they are all the same—oblivious to day and night. It is amazing how they sit with the workers and try to understand the craft of garment creation thread by thread, from *tanka* to *turpai*. It is a great indicator of their commitment to quality.

"I've seen families where the younger generation takes their ancestors' efforts for granted, squandering their wealth with abandon and bringing the family business to ruin. But here, everybody works with the same intention: to grow together. And no matter how modern the younger generation's working style may be, their basic values are drawn from one fountainhead—Kasturi Lal Jain."

Bholi
The family cook

Bholi's presence is announced even before she makes an entry. "It is best that we do the interviews in the bungalow next door," suggests a family member. "In this one, Bholi's presence will create a bit of a distraction."

Meet Bholi, and it is clear why. With her well-rounded figure, sprightly eyes and garrulous manner, she endears herself to you at once. Two things are apparent within minutes—she is a good soul, and she is inseparably bound with the Jain household.

"I first walked into *Bauji*'s household at the age of eight or nine, tagging along with my mother, who used to wash their dishes and clothes. They used to live in a four-storeyed home in Wait Gunj back then. I am just slightly older than *Bauji*'s children now, and have dedicated my life to this family.

"I also belong to the same belt as the Jains—we immigrated from Kasur after Partition. From washing clothes and *bartans*, I gradually progressed to cooking. And today, I am in charge of the kitchen as well as all the other household help. I have washed, cleaned and brought up the Jain children for two generations, and I know what each one of them likes and dislikes. From food to moods, I understand them as intimately as I do my own family.

"Their house in Wait Gunj was quite basic. *Bauji* worked day and night, and his wife did her best to support him in every way. I remember, her son Bipan was just a few months old and she needed to take rest, but she would insist on tacking labels to the mufflers on her own. Somebody warned her that all the fine work would tax her eyes, but she was determined.

"Then there were times when food was prepared from re-used cinders that had been rejected by the local press *wallah*. My little eyes saw and registered it all, imbibing with awe the quiet culture of working hard and with full honesty. Today, the family is reaping the harvest of that labour, and it makes my heart so joyful.

"Having said that, none of the prosperity and plenty has made the slightest difference in their attitude. They continue to live simply. No matter how big their current bungalows and how full their coiffeurs, they still enjoy their *khichdi* and milk.

"Perhaps the greatest learning I have got from the Jain household is the art of humility and simplicity. I am blessed to be working in a household where every family member, including the young children, practises admirable self-discipline. For example, Akhil Jain will often declare that he will eat nothing but a handful of *chana* the entire day. It requires tremendous self-control, but then that is what they are all about.

"Till today, I stitch loose pyjamas for *Bauji*. In summer, he wears them with loose *kurtas* and even steps out in them!"

The guiding light of the family, Kasturi Lal Jain has made a deep impression on the voluble Bholi. "His generosity is incredible. From a young age, I have watched him give alms and provide food to the needy. Our doors were always open for batches of barefoot saints—we would cook *phulkas* and *dal* for them morning and evening, never letting anyone leave hungry from our gates. *Bauji's* spirit of giving has ensured that his *bhandar* is always replenished with plenty."

Bholi has been with the family for more than 40 years now, and her voice chokes with emotion as she declares, "My entire life has been spent with and devoted to them. I have been trusted with the keys of the household—what can be a greater symbol of the faith they place in me? This is my world and I belong here forever."

Lal Ji Upadhyaya
Driver

A hearty laugh and a radiant personality define "Lal", as he is affectionately called. He joined Kasturi Lal Jain as a driver more than 20 years ago and simply never left. Ask him to pinpoint what made him stay, and his words flow instantly and spontaneously:

"When I began serving *Bauji*, they had a Maruti van. I was his personal driver, and privy to his daily struggles. I witnessed first-hand his incredible dedication to work, and his attention to the smallest detail. Nothing was ever too much effort for him; work came first, and took top priority in those days.

"Between then and now, the business has grown to become a virtual empire in the world of hosiery and fashion, but *Bauji's* simple ways have always remained unchanged. I remember some years ago, we went to a famous *chholey–bhature* shop in

Delhi. *Bauji* asked the stall owner to let him make his own *lassi*, and the man gladly obliged. I watched my boss stand there with a *mathni*, cheerfully churning *lassi* not only for himself but also for me and other customers. Everybody loved it! So down to earth and unassuming a man he is.

"In Tulsidas's *Ramcharitmanas*, there is a couplet that compares the elderly to children and simians. I find the truth of that reflected in *Bauji's* personality today. He is simple like a child and sometimes stubborn too! But it is always endearing, never annoying. That is also because of the deep respect he commands in our hearts.

"I came to work for him when I was a careless young man in my early twenties. I made mistakes and got roundly scolded by him, but each such scolding helped me learn and improve as both a driver and a person. Instead of sulking, I humbly asked him to slap me if I was in the wrong—for me, he has been a figure of veneration.

"Under his guidance and inspiration, I stayed firmly grounded. In the life of a driver, it is very easy to succumb to common vices such as smoking, drinking and gambling. I hail from a Brahmin family, so in many ways I was already quite pious—we did not eat meat or eggs. But *Bauji's* mentoring kept me off other bad habits, too.

"Today, I command the company's large fleet of imported and indigenous cars and two wheelers. I have earned the trust and respect of the family by staying true to my profession and values."

SECTION FIVE

JAINISM—WHAT IT IS AND WHAT IT TEACHES YOU

W HAT are the two key sects of Jainism and how are they different from each other?

The two Jain sects are the *Digambara*, meaning sky clad, and the *Shwetambara*, or the white clad. Both follow the same basic teachings and principles of Jainism, but they differ in beliefs regarding the life of Mahavira, spiritual roles, status of women, wearing of clothes for monks, rituals and texts.

Digambara

They believe that women cannot achieve liberation and be *Tirthankaras* unless they were first born as men. Their saints remain completely naked and have no worldly possessions.

In images, *Tirthankaras* have downcast eyes and are always naked.

Shwetambara

They believe *Tirthankaras* can be both men and women. Shwetambara monks wear simple white clothing and possess reading and writing materials. In images, they have prominent eyes and are always overly decorated.

Dugar Jains: The Origins[1]

The Dugar (also called Duggar, Duggad, Dugad) is a *gotra* belonging to the Jain Oswal community of Rajasthan.

The following story appears in *Mahajan Vansh Muktavali*:

The King of Maarwar, Surdeo Khich, was a brave Rajput king. He had two sons named Dugar and Sugad. Both the brothers established a new city called Aghat in Mewar. Once, criminal tribes besieged Aghat City and started killing innocent people. Both the brothers arrested and punished them. When the Nawab of Chittorgarh, Berisal Singh Sisodia, heard that Dugar and Sugad had arrested such notorious criminals, he was pleased. He called them to his palace and honoured them with the title of *Shri Raoraja*.

There was an old temple of Naharsingh Dev outside the boundary of Aghat City. Some criminal tribes around the city destroyed the temple. Dev became angry and began to create nuisance and violence in the city, started torturing and killing women and children. Despite multiple attempts, the *Raorajas* Dugar and Sugad failed to stop him.

---

1   'Dugar', Wikipedia: The Free Encyclopedia. Available at https://en.wikipedia.org/wiki/Dugar.

Then coincidentally, Manidhari Acharya Shri Jinchandra Suri came to Aghat City and was notified about the nuisance created by Dev. Acharya Shri prayed to Padmavati Devi and asked her to come and help them. Padmavati Devi appeared, captured Naharsingh Dev and killed him.

On seeing this miracle, both the brothers adopted Jainism. Manidhari Acharya Shri Jinchandra Suri made them Oswals in V.S. 1217 and their *gotras* were named Dugar and Sugad.

As they were Rajputs, Acharya Shri told them to worship Ashapura Mata as their *Kuldevi*. Her temple is situated at Nadol, Rajasthan.

Chittorgarh's Nawab Berisal Singh Sisodia was so impressed by this incident that he also became Oswal and adopted Jainism. His *gotra* was named Sisodia. His Deewaan Khetani also became Oswal, so his family was named Khetani.

In V.S. 1229, the marriage of Shri Satidas Surana's daughter Suswani was fixed with Dugar. She was beautiful, and the Nawab of Nagor heard about her and fell in love with her. He expressed his wish to marry Suswani in front of her father, but her father said that the girl was an incarnation of the Mata Ambe and it was not in his power to bestow her on anybody. The Nawab got angry and threatened to obtain her by force.

Suswani agreed to marry him on one condition: she would stand at a distance of seven feet from the Nawab and if he caught her, she would marry him. The Nawab agreed.

As per the condition, she started running on foot and Nawab followed her on horseback. He could not catch her up to Morkhana village and the distance between them remained seven feet. She kept on running and when she got tired, she went to a small shrine of Mahadev (Lord Shiva) and prayed to Mahadev to save her. Immediately, a lioness appeared, on which she mounted and entered a Kera tree. There, a chasm opened in the earth. She entered it, and it closed up again.

Soon after, Malahdas Surana, the younger brother of Shri Satidas Surana, saw a dream in which Suswani, in the form of Devi (Goddess), ordered him to construct a temple at the place where she entered the earth. When Malahdas Surana expressed the lack of money to construct the temple, Devi told him about a place with hidden treasure in his *gaushala*. Malahdas constructed a temple of Suswani Mataji with the help of that money.

Since then, Suswani Mataji is the Satimata of Dugar as well as Surana and Sankhala *gotras*. Her temple is situated at Morkhana in Bikaner district in Rajasthan.

The three categories of Dugars under the Shwetambara sect are Sthanakwasi, Terapanthi and Murtipujak.

Who are the Tirthankaras?

The Jains called their ford-makers Tirthankaras, which means a teacher who makes a way. They believe that about 24 Tirthankaras existed who attained liberation, or moksha, and taught the way to it. They were ordinary souls who achieved the highest goal of existence through meditation, penance and nature-friendly living. Therefore, a Tirthankara represents the ultimate developed state of a soul.

It is widely believed that Lord Mahavira was the founder of Jainism. The truth is that it was Lord Adinath, the first of the 24 Tirthankaras, who laid the foundations of Jainism.[2] It is believed that Lord Adinath's son, Bharat, was a Chakravarti Samrat after whom our country is named Bharat.

Tirthankaras are those who have achieved *kevala gyana*—complete knowledge of the past, present and future and the highest knowledge. Once that is achieved, they became *jinendra* or conquerors of their five senses. They are able to break free of the cycle of birth and death, attaining moksha.

Spotlight:

Lord Parshvanath: The 23rd tirthankara, Lord Parshvanath, was born in a royal family in Banaras during the 8th century. He attained *kevala gyana* after 83 days of deep meditation. During his era, the times were simpler. There was no restriction on wearing coloured clothes and jewellery, because people in general were not too materialistic. By the time the period of Lord Mahavira dawned, this had changed. He saw a great deal of avarice giving rise to malice and even violence. Gradually, the saints who followed Him began wearing only white and abandoned jewellery.

Lord Parshvanath is one of the most revered of the 24 Tirthankaras because he gave Jainism its four basic tenets:

2   Krutika Haraniya, 'The Jain Tirthankaras', *Live History India*, 25 August 2017. Available at https://www.livehistoryindia.com/story/snapshort-histories/the-jain-tirthankaras/.

Ahimsa (Non-violence), Satya (Truth), Asteya (non-stealing) and Aparigraha (non-possession). Lord Mahavira added a fifth one: Brahmacharya (continence).

How is an era defined in Jainism?

According to Jainism, an era is called a *chaubisi*, a period during which 24 Tirthankaras are honoured and followed. The *chaubisi* repeats itself infinitely, each one composed of 24 new Tirthankaras. For instance, in the next *chaubisi*, Lord Krishna and Ravana will be among the spiritual successors to the previous 24 Tirthankaras.

What are the "three jewels" of Jainism?

Samyak gyan: Right knowledge

Samyak darshan: Right belief

Samyak charitra: Right conduct

In order to attain the three jewels, every Jain should vow to five abstinences:

Ahimsa (non-violence)

Satya (truthfulness)

Asteya (no stealing)

Aparigraha (non-acquisition)

Brahmacharya (chaste living)

These vows are divided into two forms: the *Mahavrata*, which is followed by Jain monks and nuns, and the *Anuvrata*, which is the less strict version of the *Mahavrata*, followed by lay people.

The amazing life of Shwetambara Munis

An individual is recognised as a monk—*muni* or *sadhvi* in Jainism—by formally accepting *diksha*, which implies being initiated into the monastic order, or, in other words, renouncing worldly duties, possessions and family ties.

Jain monks undertake very serious forms of sacrifice. They choose a lifestyle which calls for very high control over self, to ultimately reach the supreme objective of relieving one's soul from the vicious cycle of birth, death and rebirth—*moksh*.

The life of a muni is strictly regulated by five great vows or *Mahavrata*:

1. non-violence
2. truthfulness
3. non-stealing
4. non-possession
5. chastity

Throughout their lives, they cover their bodies with white unstitched cloth, walk barefoot, do not grow their hair, eat simple food, abstain from using electricity, do not own materials, constantly practice rigorous meditation and fasting and never have physical contact with another gender.

Jain monks move in small groups of five or six, not in big monastic communities, and spend their days walking barefoot, meditating and studying. The senior monk of the group will deliver a *pravachan* each morning to an audience of monks, nuns and lay people.

The monks eat a maximum of two meals a day. They do not cook their food, nor do they get it prepared by others. Instead, they go from house to house and receive *bhiksha* from the householders. This system or practice is called *gochari*. Just as cows eat grass moving from place to place, taking little at one place and a little at another, the Jain *munis* do not take all the food from one house.

The reason Jain sadhus and sadhvis follow the practice of *gochari* is because this way the householder does not have to cook again for their needs.

They always receive food in wooden bowls and eat out of the bowls, which are called *patra*. They store boiled drinking water in clay pots. Some ascetics perform austerities and penances and hence fast for days or months on end.

Apart from this, they also practice rituals such as *Ekashana*: taking food only once a day and in one sitting only. There are some sadhus and sadhvis even today who perform *Ayambil*—a kind of austerity—continuously for several months during which they eat food only once a day.

The monks are not allowed to take a bath. This is to safeguard the life forms in the water. At the most, they can sponge themselves using boiled water.

During *chaturmas*, which coincides with the monsoon, they live in Sthanaks. After *chaturmas*, they set out for *vihar*, travelling to places chosen for them by the senior-most monks.

During *vihar*, they usually do not spend more than one day in any village on the way.

The practice of Kesh Lochan

According to the scriptures, on renouncing the world, Mahavir Bhagwan tore out his hair in five handfuls. To this day, Jain saints pluck their hair as a mark of renunciation of worldly pleasures. In the ascetic initiation carried out in Shwetamabar today, the hair is usually shaved off, apart from five small tufts that are removed by hand.

This teaches them to endure pain and is done in public with the idea of motivating the people to embark on the path of renunciation.

Samayik—A life-changing daily ritual

The Jain text *Purushartha Siddhyupaya* states the following:

After renouncing all attachments and aversions and adopting a sense of equanimity in all objects, one should practise, many times, periodic concentration (Samayik), the principal means to realise the true nature of the Self.

Samayik is the vow of periodic concentration observed by the Jains. It is one of the essential duties prescribed for both the Shravaka (householders) and ascetics. The preposition *sam* means one state of being. To become one is *Samaya*. That which has oneness as its object is Samayik, aimed at developing equanimity and refraining from injury.

"Before starting Samayik, we remove our regular clothes and wear simple but clean white cotton clothes, which are kept for Samayik only," says Neelam Jain. "We do not wear silk clothes or any leather articles, which involve much violence to bugs or animals. White is the symbol of purity and calmness and that reminds us that we should stay pure and calm."

Samayik is more than a ritual. It is a way of life, a daily practice that grounds you and fills you with positivity. No matter what your religion, the idea of setting a few minutes aside to tune out the noise of the world and tune in to yourself is a beautiful way to begin the day.

So how exactly is Samayik done? There are no hard and fast rules, but the Jain family follows this:

"Samayik is done for a period of 48 minutes. We put on simple clean white clothes and spread out an *asana* to sit on. We chant the *Namokar Mantra* on a rosary and spend time in *swadhyaya* or reading religious texts.

What are some of the things one should not do during Samayik?

Do not talk or think of anything that involves any violence.

Do not indulge in thoughts and actions that involve your business activities, family affairs and other matters.

Do not discuss, read or talk about sensual things or things related to worldly affairs.

Do not move around much—it helps you observe ahimsa (non-violence) more easily.

Do not sit in a noisy, unclean place. Select a quiet, clean place so that you are able to focus well.

This short period of prayer and mental cleansing helps you simulate the lifestyle of a saint while sitting inside your own home. Done regularly, it eventually leads you to the path of spirituality and wisdom.

This way, Samayik helps us in preventing the accumulation of new karmas and the penance we do during Samayik helps us to remove some of our accumulated karmas.

Why do Jain saints tie a white cloth around the mouth?

The white cloth mask is called a *muhapatti*. It prevents small organisms from entering the mouth and acts as a buffer so that the force of our voice and the hot air from our mouths will not kill any air beings. A *muhapatti* also prevents spit from falling on books. Another beautiful interpretation is that a white mask serves as a reminder to us that we should control what we say to others.

Why do Jain saints walk with a broom?

The broom is called *rajoharan*. It is made of fine cotton or woollen threads used to clean the floor. If for some reason someone has to walk during a Samayik then the *rajoharan* is used to wipe the floor so that no bugs are crushed.

Eight violations that are forbidden in Jainism:

1. to be disrespectful
2. to be greedy for fame and gain
3. to be proud and boastful
4. to expect rewards for kindness
5. to be rude and hurtful
6. to harbour hatred for a fellow being
7. to be lazy and sleep too much
8. to make vulgar postures

What does Samvatsari mean and how is it practised?

Samvatsari is the festival of forgiveness, celebrated by Jains on the last day of *Paryushan*, 50 days after and 70 days before the close of the *chaturmas* period.

Shwetamabar Jains celebrate *Paryushan Parva* over a period of eight days. They seek forgiveness on this auspicious day from all creatures of the world they may have hurt knowingly or unknowingly by their thoughts, words or actions, by uttering *Michhami Dukkadam*, an ancient Prakrit phrase meaning "I beg your forgiveness". People visit their friends and relatives to say *Michhami Dukkadam* and pledge that no private dispute or quarrel may be taken beyond this day of Samvatsari. On this pious day, Jains keep a fast. The next day, they take breakfast, which is known as *Parna*.

In the Digambara Jain sect, *Paryushan* is known as *Das Lakshan Parva* and it is celebrated over a period of ten days. The last day is celebrated as Samvatsari.

Namokar Mantra

This is the first prayer recited by the Jains while meditating. The mantra is also referred to as the *Pancha Namaskara Mantra*, *Navakara Mantra* or *Namaskara Mantra*.

There is no mention of any particular god or person in the *Namokar Mantra*. Instead, it focuses on the *guna* (the good qualities) of the teachers and the saints. The mantra does not ask for any favours or material benefits from the Tirthankaras or monks.

The *Namokar Mantra* simply serves as a gesture of deep respect towards beings who they believe are spiritually evolved. It also serves to remind people of their ultimate goal, i.e., *moksha*.

Namo Arihantanam: I bow down to Arihanta (souls who have reached the state of non-attachment towards worldly process).

Namo Siddhanam: I bow down to Siddha (liberated souls).

Namo Ayariyanam: I bow down to Acharya (heads of sadhus and sadhvis).

Namo Uvajjhayanam: I bow down to Upadhyaya (those who teach the scriptures).

Namo Loe Savva-sahunam: I bow down to sadhus and sadhvis (people who have renounced the material world).

Eso Panch Namokaro: These five salutations to five supreme spiritual people

Savva-pavappanasano: Destroy all sins

Manglananch Savvesim: Amongst all that is auspicious

Padhamam Havei Mangalam: This *Namokar Mantra* is the foremost.

As a gesture of goodwill for the community, the family of Kasturi Lal Jain has printed, framed and put up this mantra in more than 200 Sthanaks across India.

Jainism and food: Fascinating facts

You might have heard of Jain meals on flights and Jain *thalis* in restaurants. What this essentially means is *satvik* food without meat, eggs, onion and garlic.

Being staunch believers in *ahimsa* or non-violence, Jains do not eat meat or eggs. Plants, being *ek indriya jeev* or entities that possess only one sense, are essential to the maintenance of human life and are therefore permitted.

But even within vegetarianism, there are rules and principles. Consuming food items that may involve harming any living organism or that may induce lethargy or negativity are strictly excluded. Tubers or bulbs—veggies that grow underground, such as potatoes, onions, garlic and yams—are avoided as they have the ability to sprout and multiply. Another reason is the fact that the act of uprooting the vegetables results in harming many small insects and micro-organisms.

Alcohol and non-vegetarian food items are a strict no—no in Jainism. Fermented food items (that involve micro-organisms like yeast, bacteria to arrive at the final product) and certain bahu-beej (multi-seeded vegetables) like brinjal are also excluded. Many observe strict lacto-vegetarianism and avoid dairy consumption. Foods stored overnight or preserved for a longer period of time are also avoided. Fungi like mushrooms, fungus and yeasts do not find a place on the plate of a Jain. Honey too is forbidden, for obvious reasons.

Food is not eaten after sunset. It should only be eaten during sunlight hours. Micro-organisms grow on food after sunset. The digestive system also remains in good health if food is eaten during the day.

Fasting

The Jain focus on fasting becomes clearer when one looks at the examples and reasoning provided within Jain literature. Fasting is a critical part of Jain spiritual pursuit, and Mahavira himself is said to have fasted for extraordinarily long periods. Jain festivals incorporate fasting as a central element, as does all of Jain mythology.

Meditative fasting itself is said to generate inner spiritual heat, which quickens the process of ripening and dissolution of existing bondages of the soul. Often, the merits of various good actions are measured by scaling them against the merit one would acquire by fasting for a number of days.

Even amongst contemporary Jain laypeople, frequent or occasional fasting is very common as a part of tradition, spiritual practice and routine life.

In Kasturi Lal Jain's household, fasts are observed regularly, even by the children of the family. The nature of the fasts varies, but they are usually one-day fasts such as *Ekashana*, during which only one meal is eaten while sitting in one position or asana. Then there is *Ayambil*, another one-day fast during which the family practises self-control by eating only one meal and that too without any added flavour or fat. That meal could be just a handful of boiled grains, minus salt or spices. There are fasts that allow only a 48-minute window for the consumption of simple food. All of these have one key thread in common—the practice of sensory control and spiritual evolvement.

Quotes to be sprinkled across the book:

➤ "For those who have steadied their minds with yoga and absorbed themselves into meditation, there is no difference between a crowd and a quiet village."

➤ "A pitcher full of water is silent. One which is only half full makes a noise. Similarly, the truly learned and evolved do not boast."

➤ "Which enemy can destroy one who holds the weapon of forgiveness? Even a raging fire dies out if it falls on a spot where there is no hay."

➤ "The jewel of human life is beauty. The jewel of beauty is character. The jewel of character is knowledge. And the jewel of knowledge is forgiveness."

➤ "Everywhere that the footsteps of the great *gurus* fall, beautiful blossoms of joy spring up."